·80· GREAT
NATURAL
GARDEN
PLANTS

·80· GREAT
NATURAL
GARDEN
PLANTS

KEN DRUSE

CLARKSON POTTER/PUBLISHERS
NEW YORK

The photographs in this book were previously published in *The Natural Garden* by Ken Druse.

Grateful acknowledgment is given for permission to reprint the following photographs: page 10: Mark Hulla; page 11: Jerry Harpur; page 66 center: Michael Dirr; pages 82 middle and 106 top right: Lisa Dreishpoon; page 106 bottom right: William Mills

Published by Clarkson N. Potter, Inc., 201 East 50th Street, New York, New York 10022. Member of the Crown Publishing Group.

Random House, Inc. New York, Toronto, London, Sydney, Auckland

http://www.randomhouse.com/

CLARKSON POTTER, POTTER, and colophon are trademarks of Crown Publishers, Inc.

Printed in Hong Kong

Library of Congress Cataloging-in-Publication Data is available upon request

ISBN 0-609-80042-6

10 9 8 7 6 5 4 3 2 1

First Edition

Acknowledgments

I want to thank some of the people who helped produce this book: Chip Gibson, President and Publisher of Crown Publishers; Lauren Shakely, Clarkson Potter's Editorial Director, who suggested this project and made this idea into reality; Maggie Hinders, the book designer, whose contribution is obvious; Lisa Sloane, who assisted with design; and Mark McCauslin, production editor, and Joan Denman, production manager. Their less visible work was equally important.

I want to thank Laurie Stark, Joan De Mayo, Tina Constable, and Mary Ellen Briggs for always doing more than their share on our projects. I am especially grateful to my editor, Eliza Scott. Thanks also to Helen Pratt, my indefatigable agent; Louis Bauer for his patience; and George Waffle for his friendship and efforts. I also must thank Ruth Clausen, whose help in making this book accurate and useful was invaluable.

Lastly, I have to thank you. As I travel and lecture around the country, it is so gratifying to learn that my books have helped (and touched) so many.

The plants I've chosen are presented with their cousins and intimate friends from the botanical community—in all, hundreds to collect and grow.

Contents

Introduction

The natural garden has become the new American gardening style. It is informal—planned, but without being self-conscious. It reflects nature in its design and respects nature by forgoing the use of potentially hazardous chemicals. Rather than taking inspiration from the gardening styles of other countries, like formal French, English, or Japanese gardens, we look to our local surroundings as sources for design.

North America has some of the most remarkable plant community types and topographical characteristics of any place on earth. In the temperate world, the southeastern states are second only to China in native plant diversity, and the canyons of the Southwest and big-tree forests of the Northwest have no parallel on earth.

Although they cannot re-create the best nature has to offer, gardens can remind us of the few wild places left, and also include some local plants whose own habitats are endangered by development. Some of us gardeners are also activists, literally racing ahead of the bulldozer on organized plant-rescue missions to dig up and relocate species in its path.

Besides being earth-friendly, ecologically correct, and organic, natural gardens are people-friendly and easy on the eye, reflecting the needs of the people who use and enjoy them. Think of your property in terms of three general areas: the inner area close to the house; the outer area along the edges of the property; and the places in between. These divisions, though not necessarily strict demarcations, will help you think of the best way to use the landscape and the ways you can make this use comfortable and efficient.

The inner area is often the most developed space, with places for recreation, entertaining, and utility, such as an out-of-sight spot for the trash can and a direct path to the electric meter. If you decide to pave some of this area, use a material that comes from the earth, such as wood, stone, or clay bricks. Whenever possible, avoid mortar. Bricks and stones should be set in sand so that rain water can percolate down to the soil below. Air will come up to keep this patch of earth from suffocating. As for asphalt, there is enough of that in America already, don't you think?

The outer area is the most relaxed and informal place, often serving as a sight and sound barrier from neighboring houses. A background of trees and shrubs is not only beautiful, but also adds oxygen to the surroundings and provides cooling shade. It can be 15°F. cooler in the shade in summer than in the open. Shade also affords an opportunity to grow some of the most exquisite jewels of the botanical kingdom—the woodland ephemerals, like *Trillium*, Virginia bluebells, and Jack-in-the-pulpit.

The in-between area is the place to let your horticultural imagination run wild. You should reduce your lawn to the amount needed for recreation. Lawn is alive—it breathes and is home to countless organisms, but it is an unnatural contrivance tied to a life of perpetual care. In order for the grass to be usable as lawn, it must be mowed. In order to keep it green, it must be watered and fed, which makes it grow faster and require more mowing. It devours all kinds of resources: water, petroleum, and human energy.

Water is about the most precious of our natural resources and must be respected. Whatever happens in gardening in the future, I know that there is a finite amount of water, and always more people who need to use it. Water, and often the lack of it, will ultimately determine what the gardens of the next millennium will be like. That does not mean you have to grow only cacti. Look around you on the roadside at the woods, prairie, and mountains, places with plants that thrive with no extra irrigation from anybody. The plants that grow there have evolved to be self-sufficient, another reason to adopt the most friendly approach to gardening and welcome the native plants to our homesite.

Instead of having a lawn or energy-guzzling formal plantings, give over some in-between area to meadow. Make a self-contained perennial bed of drought-resistant plants. Create a flower border or garden pool with a pump that recirculates water (nothing attracts birds like moving water). Grow vegetables in a patch, raised bed, or containers where their needs can be met. Make a mini-orchard. Anything, as long as you consider that the most important maintenance task is to sustain the health of the earth.

In 1981, I wrote that natural gardens are made in partnership with nature. Since then, this has been repeated in scores of books, magazines, and newspaper articles. Now this guide will help you to select some of the best plants and their design companions with descriptions and cultural information to help them thrive in your natural garden. Be sure to take it with you to the nursery or garden. There is nothing that thrills me more than to see a well-worn copy of one of my books.

Annuals

Annuals

An annual is a plant that lives a year, at most—sometimes just a season. In this short life, these plants have to bloom, be fertilized, make seeds, and deliver or disperse them to a safe place. The need to attract pollinators in a hurry necessitates great color, form, and fragrance—an irresistible hook.

If you have a meadow or prairie planting, you might throw in the seeds of some colorful annuals to make a quick splash in the early days before the perennials get established, as perennials usually do not bloom the first season from seed. Scatter some California poppy seeds in the late winter for funnel-shaped orange flowers that spring. Sow seeds in early spring for summer annuals like pink or sherbert-orange cosmos, blue bachelor buttons, annual black-eyed Susans, golden sunflowers, and orange Mexican sunflowers. Most annuals want as much sun as possible.

The demand and supply for subtle annuals have increased in the last few years. There's *Zinnia linearus* (*Z. angustifolia*), a sensational plant from Mexico with needlelike leaves and white or yellow daisylike flowers. They creep and are excellent for hanging baskets in the sun, to jazz up the front edge of a planting, or to trail over and soften the rim of a half-whiskey barrel. Seek out some of the species marigold cultivars such as my favorite *Tagetes tenuifolia*, 'Lemon Gem', which grows into 1- to 1½-foot-tall "shrubs" of feathery foliage covered with tiny, pale yellow single flowers. Although not new, the delicate *Cleome*, spider flower, presents another version of subtlety, with 5-inch flower heads made up of many intricate individual blossoms.

But many of us do want the punchy color annuals can provide, such as the globe amaranth with hundreds of thimble-shaped flowers in vivid colors. If picked and dried, they will last inside for years. There's something for everyone.

Fragrance is the final attribute. Among the best are the flowering tobaccos, nicotianas; avoid the modern hybrids, many of which have no scent. The original species, *Nicotiana alata*, still smells best, but look for *N. langsdorffi* with tiny, chartreuse, nodding, urn-shaped flowers, and *N. sylvestris*, with giant, 4-inch-long, night-scented tubes for flowers, which attract nocturnal pollinators like moths.

Centaurea cyanus
(bachelor's button,
cornflower)

Cleome hasslerana 'Helen
Campbell' (spider flower)

Coreopsis tinctoria
(calliopsis)

LEFT
Cosmos bipinnatus
(pink cosmos)

CENTAUREA CYANUS

PRONUNCIATION: sen-TOR-ee-a sy-AN-us
COMMON NAME: Bachelor's button,
cornflower
HOMELAND: Southeastern Europe
HARDINESS: Hardy annual
SIZE: 15"–36" tall; 6"–8" across

INTEREST: Single or double flowers in deep
blue, white, pink, or purple on tall stems in
early summer. Often self-sows.
LIGHT CONDITIONS: Full sun to partial shade
SOIL/MOISTURE: Well-drained, average to
poor soil

DESCRIPTION: Before the days of herbicides, this old-fashioned annual often grew alongside oats, barley, or wheat in the cornfields of Europe. It is seldom seen today, but it is still popular in cottage and cutting gardens and is often a component of meadow-garden seed mixes. For natural-looking results, broadcast-sow cornflowers direct as soon as the soil is workable in spring (or in fall in appropriate climates). The numerous named cultivars and strains include the 16"–tall Polka Dot Hybrids strain in reds, pinks, lavenders, and white. Combine with annual coreopsis, red poppies, and white daisies or cosmos.

CLEOME HASSLERANA [C. spinosa hort.]

PRONUNCIATION: klee-OH-me hass-ler-AN-h
COMMON NAME: Spider flower
HOMELAND: West Indies; cultivar of garden
origin
HARDINESS: Half-hardy annual
SIZE: 3'–5' tall; 12"–24" across

INTEREST: Large columnar heads of delicate
white (or shades of pink through purple)
flowers atop strong leafy stems
LIGHT CONDITIONS: Full sun to light shade
SOIL/MOISTURE: Average soil; tolerates dry-
ness once established.

DESCRIPTION: These airy flowers are attractive among shrubs and foundation plantings and are often seen in cottage-style gardens. White 'Helen Campbell' is spectacular against a background of dark evergreens but is equally lovely with frosty artemisias or variegated grasses. The more compact Queen strain has flowers in pinks, white, and violet, but cultivars are available in separate colors, e.g., 'Rose Queen'. Excellent as a cut flower and attractive to hummingbirds. Self-sows. The common name may come from the seed pods that stick out like legs all around the stalk.

COREOPSIS TINCTORIA

PRONUNCIATION: ko-ree-OP-sis tink-TOR-ree-a

COMMON NAME: Calliopsis

HOMELAND: Native; Minnesota to Arizona

HARDINESS: Hardy annual

SIZE: 8"–36" tall; 12"–15" across

INTEREST: Yellow to maroon, sometimes bicolored, 2" daisy flowers most of the summer

LIGHT CONDITIONS: Full sun to very light shade

SOIL/MOISTURE: Average to poor soil with good drainage

DESCRIPTION: This underused prairie annual is a source of yellow or burnt orange dye, which gives rise to another common name, dyer's coreopsis. Calliopsis is excellent in meadows and in wild and native-plant gardens, where it self-sows freely; a popular component of meadow seed mixes. Good for cutting and as a companion for other annuals and perennials in the flower border. Seeds of the species display a range of color forms; cultivars include 'Atropurpurea', which has dark crimson flowers, and compact 'Nana', which seldom exceeds 8". Very long-blooming, except in hot, humid climates, where *Bidens* spp. would make a good replacement.

COSMOS BIPINNATUS

PRONUNCIATION: KOS-mos bi-pin-AY-tus

COMMON NAME: Pink cosmos

HOMELAND: Mexico

HARDINESS: Tender annual

SIZE: To 6' tall; 15"–18" across

INTEREST: Pink, white, or crimson daisies up to 4" across, all summer on sturdy stems clothed with fernlike foliage

LIGHT CONDITIONS: Full sun to light shade

SOIL/MOISTURE: Well-drained soil of average to poor fertility

DESCRIPTION: This easy-to-grow annual has rightly become one of the most popular annuals for American gardens. At home in meadow gardens, with sunflowers, or in a more formal flower border with love-lies-bleeding or zinnias, long-blooming pink cosmos always carries its weight. The tall varieties, picked early in the day, make excellent cut flowers. Deadhead routinely to extend season. There are several reliable strains: Sonata series, which tops at 2' tall; Sea Shells Mix, which has tubular flowers on 4' stems; and semidouble Psyche Mix, which is about 3' tall.

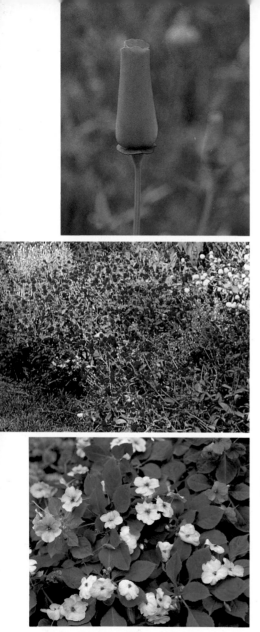

Eschscholzia californica
(California poppy)

Gomphrena globosa
(globe amaranth)

Impatiens wallerana
(impatiens, busy Lizzie)

RIGHT
Rudbeckia hirta (black-eyed
Susan, gloriosa daisy)

ESCHSCHOLZIA CALIFORNICA

PRONUNCIATION: esh-SHOLT-zee-a kal-i-FORN-ik-a

COMMON NAME: California poppy

HOMELAND: Native; California

HARDINESS: Hardy annual

SIZE: 12"–18" tall; 6"–10" across

INTEREST: In spring, flaring bowl-shaped flowers to 4" in vivid orange open above ferny blue-green foliage when the sun is shining.

LIGHT CONDITIONS: Full sun

SOIL/MOISTURE: Free-draining sandy soil, neutral to alkaline

DESCRIPTION: In the wild, the state flower of California paints hillsides with brilliant orange, often highlighted with blue lupines. Mass in meadow gardens with bachelor's buttons, Texas bluebonnets, or annual larkspur; regularly included in commercial meadow seed mixes. California poppies are also suitable in rock gardens or along paths as an edging; sow directly and thin to 6" apart. Modern strains expand the color range and include Thai Silk, which bears semidouble flowers of pinks, reds, and orange; and Monarch Mix, which has single and semidouble flowers from pale cream through yellow and orange to deep reds. Self-seeds, but the strains will not come true.

GOMPHRENA GLOBOSA

PRONUNCIATION: gom-FREE-na glow-BOW-sa

COMMON NAME: Globe amaranth

HOMELAND: Central America

HARDINESS: Tender annual

SIZE: 8"–3' tall; 12" or so across

INTEREST: Cloverlike heads of flowers in white, red, purple, lavender, and sometimes orange, summer to fall frosts

LIGHT CONDITIONS: Full sun

SOIL/MOISTURE: Well-drained, fertile soil that does not dry out excessively

DESCRIPTION: Globe amaranth is excellent massed but also looks attractive grouped with perennials and other annuals. 'Strawberry Fields' ['Strawberry Fayre'] has scarlet flowers on 18"–24" stems and excels in hot-colored designs, perhaps with calliopsis (*Zinnia augustifolia*) or 'Stella d'Oro' daylily. 'Lavender Lady' is an attractive soft lavender; accent with *Verbena bonariensis* or lavender petunias. The 24" Pomponette strain is available in separate colors. 'Dwarf Buddy', which offers magenta flowers on 8" plants, is suitable for edgings or in containers. All cut and dry well. Water during dry spells to minimize mildew.

IMPATIENS WALLERANA

PRONUNCIATION: im-PAY-shens wol-er-AN-a
COMMON NAME: Impatiens, busy Lizzie
HOMELAND: Of garden origin
HARDINESS: USDA Zones 10–11
SIZE: 6″–18″ tall; to 18″ across
INTEREST: Slightly puckered green leaves with clusters of 1″ flat flowers nestling atop each stem
LIGHT CONDITIONS: Light shade to shade
SOIL/MOISTURE: Well-drained, but moisture-retentive soil of average to rich fertility. They must not dry out.

DESCRIPTION: This tender perennial, treated as an annual in all but the mildest parts of the country, is grown by the acre in public and private gardens nationwide. The double-flowered forms have only recently been on the market, and though attractive massed, they deserve to be admired close up in a special container, rock garden, or raised bed. Sometimes, the bright colors of these flowers can be a bit much for a natural garden. Avoid mixing plants with many colors, and also look for the "Hawaiian" impatiens with many small flowers along 1½′ tall stems, which look best in naturalistic plantings.

RUDBECKIA HIRTA

PRONUNCIATION: rood-BEK-ee-a HER-ta
COMMON NAME: Black-eyed Susan, gloriosa daisy
HOMELAND: Native; western Massachusetts to Illinois, south to Georgia and Alabama
HARDINESS: Biennial, treated as a half-hardy annual
SIZE: To 3′ tall; 12″–15″ across
INTEREST: Coarse, hairy foliage with large yellow daisies, centered with a black or dark brown cone. Flowers in early to mid-summer.
LIGHT CONDITIONS: Full sun
SOIL/MOISTURE: Rich or average to even poor, well-drained soil

DESCRIPTION: Spectacular massed alone or with daylilies, black-eyed Susan is also useful in cutting gardens, cottage-style and meadow or wild gardens, and in more formal beds and borders with other annuals, perennials, and evergreens. The Rustic Dwarfs strain grows 2′ tall with 3″ flowers in yellow, orange, and mahogany. Up to 3′ tall, the long-blooming Indian Summer strain has huge 6″–9″ golden daisies shaded with light brown. 'Double Gold' has semidouble, rich yellow 4″ flowers; compact 15″ 'Goldilocks' also has 3″–4″ blooms. Water during dry spells for best results, although will tolerate drought; be alert for slugs.

Myosotis alpestris
(forget-me-not)

Salvia farinacea 'Victoria'
(mealycup sage)

Tithonia rotundifolia
(Mexican sunflower)

LEFT
Tropaeolum majus
'Nanum' (nasturtium)

MYOSOTIS ALPESTRIS

PRONUNCIATION: my-o-SO-tis al-PEST-ris
COMMON NAME: Forget-me-not
HOMELAND: Europe; strains of garden origin
HARDINESS: Hardy biennial
SIZE: 6″–24″ tall; clumps 12″ across
INTEREST: Sometimes pink or white, but mostly brilliant blue, tiny forget-me-not flowers with a yellow eye in mid- to late spring
LIGHT CONDITIONS: Light to partial shade, especially in hot regions
SOIL/MOISTURE: Moist but not waterlogged soil, amended with compost or leaf mold

DESCRIPTION: Although listed under this species, most biennial forget-me-nots probably fall under *M. sylvatica*. They are superb for providing a second tier of color underplanting tulips, daffodils, and other spring bulbs, as well as for lining pathways and along woodland streams. Good for spring containers. In woodlands mix with creeping phlox, columbines, and spring ephemerals; an elegant underplanting for ostrich ferns. Several strains are available. Self-seeds freely; remove spent plants. Susceptible to mildew if stressed by drought.

SALVIA FARINACEA 'VICTORIA'

PRONUNCIATION: SAL-vee-a fa-rin-AY-cee-a
COMMON NAME: Mealycup sage
HOMELAND: Native; Texas; cultivar of garden origin
HARDINESS: Tender perennial treated as an annual
SIZE: 18″–24″ tall; 12″–18″ across
INTEREST: Silver foliage with spires of violet-blue or white flowers most of the season
LIGHT CONDITIONS: Full sun to very light shade
SOIL/MOISTURE: Well-drained, moist soil

DESCRIPTION: Mealycup sage is a standby of summer and early-fall borders. The tall cultivars are bold enough to plant among shrubs or foundation plantings, while all pair well with other annuals and perennials. Be sure to plant enough of these narrow plants to make a show—they are wonderful as a stream of blue. Useful as a cut flower, mealycup sage retains its color when dried. 'Victoria' is an 18″ cultivar with 8″ or longer spikes of deep blue flowers; 24″-tall 'Blue Bedder' is a darker blue. Widely grown 'White Porcelain' reaches 18″ tall. Mealycup sage is attractive to honeybees, butterflies. and hummingbirds.

Tithonia rotundifolia

PRONUNCIATION: tith-OH-nee-a roe-tun-dif-FOE-lee-a

COMMON NAME: Mexican sunflower

HOMELAND: Mexico

HARDINESS: Tender annual

SIZE: To 6' or more, 24"–36" across

INTEREST: Rich orange daisies, 3" or more across, on tall plants, clothed with somewhat coarse leaves. Flowers mid-summer to fall.

LIGHT CONDITIONS: Full sun

SOIL/MOISTURE: Well-drained, average soil. Avoid rich or wet soil.

DESCRIPTION: Mexican sunflower is a giant for the back of flower borders or along the spine of island beds. Ideal in front of evergreens or between foundation plantings and even useful as a screen. Combine it with vibrant purple *Salvia leucantha* or *Buddleia davidii* 'Black Knight'. Mexican sunflowers are attractive to butterflies and hummingbirds. They tolerate heat, humidity, and even seasonal drought. Scarlet 'Torch' and chrome 'Yellow Torch' may top 4'; 'Goldfinger', at 3' tall, is more in scale with smaller gardens. Rich soil encourages huge, lush plants at the expense of flowers.

Tropaeolum majus 'Nanum'

PRONUNCIATION: troe-PEE-o-lum MAY-jus

COMMON NAME: Nasturtium

HOMELAND: Mexico to Peru; cultivar of garden origin

HARDINESS: Hardy annual

SIZE: 1'–4' tall; 12"–15" across

INTEREST: Quantities of 2"–3" funnel-shaped, spurred flowers in bright reds, yellows, and orange in summer; winter and spring in hot climates

LIGHT CONDITIONS: Full sun

SOIL/MOISTURE: Average to poor, well-drained soil. Avoid rich soil, which encourages leafy growth but few flowers.

DESCRIPTION: Many strains and cultivars are on the market. 'Nanum' is a non-climbing dwarf, with smaller flowers than some; it is ideal for container culture, as are plants of the Jewel series. The Gleam varieties sprawl or are semitrailing, good for hanging baskets. White-splashed 'Alaska' is grown as a foliage plant. Both single- and double-flowered sorts are available, most offering fragrant flowers in countless shades of red, yellow, orange, and even cream; 'Moonlight' is a cool pale yellow. An easy, cheerful plant, nasturtium blooms brighten any part of sunny gardens and are a stylish garnish for summer salads.

Perennials

Perennials

Although annuals may possess big flashes of color for longer periods through the season, perennials are the plants —colors, if you will—from which you can create your most exquisite, enduring garden paintings. You could create a planting with perennials in shades as hot as any red, orange, or yellow annual's, or, as many people choose to do, plan for a more subdued color scheme—perhaps a gradation from pink to mauve to blue. Try planting a perennial border in a ribbon of color, which may be just right to soften the lines of a wall. Nothing enhances a border like a background to stop the eye from drifting beyond the plants.

Another option is to create an island in the middle of the lawn, with the tallest plants in the center. Start by eliminating the grass. One way is to kill it with a technique called solarization. Cover the planting area with a plastic sheet for several months in warm weather, which essentially cooks the grass and any weeds or weed seeds with it. In my new garden, I have done different things with sod. In some places, I sliced it off to a depth of about 3 inches and turned it grass-side down. This will kill most of the grass, but keep the soil and nutrients in place. You'll have to let it sit for a while to dry and decompose.

In one area, I covered the sod with newspaper that I wet to keep from blowing away, and followed this with a layer of well-composted manure or clean top soil. In another area, I harvested the sod, cutting it off and placing it on a concrete bridge faced on the ends with stone. The perennial plantings around the bridge include an herb collection at one corner; moisture-loving plants at another. Across from these is a planting of silver and blue plants— hostas, artemesias, mountain mint, *Rudbeckia maxima.* The shaded fourth corner is home to hardy geraniums and yellow poppies.

A less conventional way to use perennials is in a meadow or prairie planting with Joe Pye weed, thinleaf sunflower, blazing star, *Rudbeckia,* goldenrod, and beebalm allowed to naturalize and fill in the spaces. The meadow is a mainstay of the natural garden that will attract desirable critters such as songbirds and butterflies.

Achillea species
(yarrow)

Ajuga pyramidalis
(upright bugleweed)

Arisaema triphyllum
(Jack-in-the-pulpit)

RIGHT
Aquilegia hybrid
(columbine)

ACHILLEA SPECIES

PRONUNCIATION: a-kil-LEE-a

COMMON NAME: Yarrow

HOMELAND: North temperate regions of the world; cultivars of garden origin

HARDINESS: USDA Zones 3–9

SIZE: 6"–36" tall; 12"–36" across

INTEREST: Typically fernlike divided leaves, often silvery, with flattish heads of yellow, white, or red flowers in late spring and summer

LIGHT CONDITIONS: Full sun to very light shade

SOIL/MOISTURE: Average to poor, well-drained soil

DESCRIPTION: Yarrows are invaluable in sunny flower borders and are excellent as fresh or dried cut flowers. Among the most popular are the hybrid *A.* × 'Coronation Gold', which has 3"–4" heads of brilliant yellow flowers on strong 2'–3' stems; paler yellow, 1'–2'-tall *A.* × 'Moonshine' also has gray-green foliage. Common yarrow, *A. millefolium,* has white or cerise flowers and spreads quickly; 'Cerise Queen' is a favorite 18" cultivar. The newly introduced Galaxy hybrids are available in pale yellows, rich reds, and paprika as well as in peach and salmon shades.

AJUGA PYRAMIDALIS

PRONUNCIATION: a-JEW-gah peer-am-id-AH-lis

COMMON NAME: Upright bugleweed

HOMELAND: Europe

HARDINESS: USDA Zones 3–9

SIZE: 6"–9" tall; spreading 12" across

INTEREST: Mats of slightly glossy leaves, above which rise plump spikes of deep Wedgwood-blue flowers in mid-spring

LIGHT CONDITIONS: Full sun to partial shade

SOIL/MOISTURE: Moisture-retentive but not soggy, average soil

DESCRIPTION: Not as spreading as carpet or common bugleweed, upright bugleweed is better suited to small gardens where space is at a premium. Attractive under high-pruned trees, along pathways, and as an underplanting for rhododendrons and other shrubs. Plant miniature daffodils underneath for a cheerful blue-and-yellow spring combination. Cut spent flower spikes to the ground for neatness. 'Metallica Crispa' has crinkled, reddish brown leaves that glint in the sun, but it can get badly infested with aphids.

AQUILEGIA HYBRID McKANA GIANTS STRAIN

PRONUNCIATION: ack-wil-LEE-jee-a ×
HIB-rid

COMMON NAME: Columbine

HOMELAND: Of garden origin

HARDINESS: USDA Zones 3—9

SIZE: 18″—30″ tall; 15″—18″ across

INTEREST: Attractive compound leaves, often
bluish green, above which dance dainty,
long-spurred, 1″—2″ blossoms, in all colors.
Flowers in late spring.

LIGHT CONDITIONS: Full sun to open shade,
as cast by buildings

SOIL/MOISTURE: Well-drained, rich soil,
amended with compost or leaf mold

DESCRIPTION: Columbines are indispensable in early-summer flower beds and borders, cottage gardens, light woodlands, and even meadow gardens in cool regions. The elegant McKana Giants have very large flowers in all shades, mostly pastel, and often bicolored. They combine well with early soft pink alliums and late-blooming tulips as well as bold-leaved hostas and strap-leaved lilyturf in shaded spots. Leaf miner is a disfiguring problem in many gardens; cut the foliage to the ground to encourage fresh young growth, which will remain attractive for many weeks. Columbines are short-lived at best, so start new seeds every couple of years to keep young replacements in the wings.

ARISAEMA TRIPHYLLUM

PRONUNCIATION: a-riss-EE-ma tri-FILL-um

COMMON NAME: Jack-in-the-pulpit

HOMELAND: Native; northeastern U.S., south
to North Carolina and west to Kansas

HARDINESS: USDA Zones 4—9

SIZE: 12″—15″ tall; 12″ across

INTEREST: Three-parted leaves, each leaflet
2″—3″ long. Curious spring blossom, with a
central green or purplish spadix surrounded
by a hooded purple-striped or pale green
spathe. Red berries form on the spadix after
the minute female flowers are fertilized.

LIGHT CONDITIONS: Light shade to shade

SOIL/MOISTURE: Rich, moisture-retentive
soil, amended with compost or leaf mold

DESCRIPTION: This native woodland plant is one of our most easily recognized eastern spring ephemerals. Its unusual inflorescence attracts attention from those who appreciate the subtleties of green flowers. The starchy tubers were cooked by Native Americans, inspiring another common name, Indian turnip. Suitable in wild and native-plant gardens as well as in woodland areas. Offered mostly by native-plant specialty nurseries, and easy to grow from seeds washed of berry pulp and sown.

Astilbe chinensis 'Pumila'
(Chinese astilbe)

Baptisia australis
(wild blue indigo)

Chrysanthemum × *superbum*
[*Leucanthemum* × *superbum*]
(Shasta daisy)

LEFT
Dicentra spectabilis
(bleeding heart)

ASTILBE CHINENSIS 'PUMILA'

PRONUNCIATION: as-TIL-bee chin-EN-sis
COMMON NAME: Chinese astilbe
HOMELAND: China; cultivar of garden origin
HARDINESS: USDA Zones 3–8
SIZE: 12"–18" tall; spreading to 2' across
INTEREST: Dense spikes of crushed-raspberry-colored flowers in summer. Bronze, deeply cut leaves
LIGHT CONDITIONS: Light to medium shade
SOIL/MOISTURE: Moisture-retentive, organic soil, enriched with plenty of manure, compost, or leaf mold. Keep constantly moist.

DESCRIPTION: Although variable in height, 'Pumila' is perhaps the best of the false spireas to use as a ground-cover plant. It spreads readily and effectively chokes out weeds under shrubs and foundation plantings. Allow the spent cinnamon-colored flower spikes to remain on the plants into the winter, for interest during the dark days. Another dwarf astilbe to watch for is *A.* 'sprite' with airy, delicate, pale pink flower spikes.

BAPTISIA AUSTRALIS

PRONUNCIATION: bap-TIZ-ee-a ows-TRAH-lis
COMMON NAME: Wild blue indigo
HOMELAND: Native; Pennsylvania to Georgia and Indiana
HARDINESS: USDA Zones 3–9
SIZE: 3'–5' tall; 3'–4' across
INTEREST: Straight stems grow into shrubby masses of compound leaves with spikes of purplish blue pea flowers in late spring
LIGHT CONDITIONS: Full sun to light shade
SOIL/MOISTURE: Deep, well-drained soil, enriched with compost or leaf mold

DESCRIPTION: Although this native seldom blooms for more than 2 weeks, its bold proportions warrant a place in perennial and mixed gardens as well as in informal spaces devoted to native plants. Combine it with blue or white Siberian iris or carpet its feet with coralbells for a late-spring display. After bloom, trim it into a shapely mound to provide structure through the summer. The slightly bluish leaves make a nice background for lively coreopsis, zinnias, petunias, marigolds, and other bright annuals. If plants are left unpruned, the seedpods mature to an interesting dark brown or black and make unusual additions to dried wreaths and winter bouquets. Avoid staking if possible, or install supports early enough that the plant outgrows them.

CHRYSANTHEMUM × SUPERBUM

PRONUNCIATION: kris-SAN-the-mum × sue-PUR-bum

COMMON NAME: Shasta daisy

HOMELAND: Of garden origin

HARDINESS: USDA Zones 5–9

SIZE: 1'–3' tall; to 2' across

INTEREST: Dark green, toothed foliage and numerous daisylike flowers to 5" across

LIGHT CONDITIONS: Full sun or light shade

SOIL/MOISTURE: Well-drained, fertile soil

DESCRIPTION: What cottage garden or garden for cut flowers could do without Shasta daisies? Long grown by cottagers for their ease of culture, they have been adopted by the florist industry and are often dyed hideous colors. In the garden their pristine white heads, sometimes semidouble or double, grace beds and borders alongside shrubs, annuals and other perennials. Mass them or group them for best effect. Short-lived, especially in warm climates, it is best to divide every 2–3 years to maintain vigor. Reliable cultivars include semidouble 'Little Miss Muffet', which seldom tops 12" tall; single-flowered 'Super Alaska', which may reach 3'; and double-flowered 'Aglaya', which rises 18"–24".

DICENTRA SPECTABILIS

PRONUNCIATION: dy-SEN-tra spek-TAH-bi-lis

COMMON NAME: Bleeding heart

HOMELAND: Japan

HARDINESS: USDA Zones 2–9

SIZE: 2'–3' tall; spreading about 18" across

INTEREST: Loose mounds of divided leaves. The heart-shaped, 1" flowers, pink or white, are borne along one side of the gently arching and rather brittle stems, looking much like valentines strung in a row.

LIGHT CONDITIONS: Partial shade

SOIL/MOISTURE: Moisture-retentive, organic soil, amended with compost or leaf mold

DESCRIPTION: A favorite of gardeners for generations, bleeding heart somehow captures the romance of gardening. In most climates the foliage yellows and dies back after bloom, leaving an awkward hole in the border. Interplant with other perennials, especially ferns or hostas, which will grow into the gap. Underplant with spring bulbs, perhaps a pink narcissus such as 'Pink Champion'; *D. s.* 'Alba' looks good with Narcissus 'Thalia' or 'Ice Follies'. *D.S.*'s american cousins include eastern *D. eximis* and western *D. formosa*. These, although less romantic, perhaps, bloom spring to fall if nights are cool.

Eupatorium maculatum
(Joe Pye weed)

Helianthus decapetalus
(thinleaf sunflower)

Helleborus argutifolius
(Corsican hellebore)

RIGHT
Hemerocallis × *hybrida*
(daylily)

EUPATORIUM MACULATUM

PRONUNCIATION: yew-pa-TOR-ee-um mac-yew-LAY-tum

COMMON NAME: Joe Pye weed

HOMELAND: Native; New England to North Carolina and New Mexico

HARDINESS: USDA Zones 2–9

SIZE: 4'–7' tall; 3' or so across

INTEREST: Tall speckled stems, clothed with whorls of rough, vanilla-scented leaves and topped with compound heads of tiny, dusty purple flowers in late summer.

LIGHT CONDITIONS: Full sun

SOIL/MOISTURE: Moisture-retentive or even wet soil of average fertility

DESCRIPTION: This tall native is at its best planted in large groups beside ponds or lakes, where the soil remains damp. It is also appropriate at the edge of damp woodlands, perhaps with shrubby summersweet, and in native-plant or wild gardens. In the flower garden, Joe Pye weed makes a fine background or screen and combines well with New York ironweed and tall asters. Attractive to butterflies. Recently introduced *E.* 'Gateway' with truer flower color and near-black stems tops at 5'—more in scale for gardens where space is limited.

HELIANTHUS DECAPETALUS

PRONUNCIATION: hee-lee-AN-thus dek-a-PET-al-us

COMMON NAME: Thinleaf sunflower

HOMELAND: Native; northeastern states to the Great Plains

HARDINESS: USDA Zones 5–9

SIZE: 4'–5' or more tall; 18"–30" across

INTEREST: Masses of bright yellow daisy flowers on tall stems from summer into fall

LIGHT CONDITIONS: Full sun

SOIL/MOISTURE: Well-drained soil of average fertility

DESCRIPTION: These tall, cheerful plants seem to embody the spirit of the plains. Mass them in an open meadow, or on the high bank of a pond or lake, where their reflection can be seen. In a flower border, it is wiser to use a slightly less invasive cultivar of the hybrid *H.* × *multiflorus*, of which thinleaf sunflower is a parent. 'Loddon Gold', which has double pompom flowers 2"–5" across, and earlier-blooming 'Flore Pleno' are frequently offered. 'Capenoch Star' has less brassy, single flowers. All should be divided every 2–3 years to curtail the roots and to encourage abundant flowers.

HELLEBORUS ARGUTIFOLIUS

PRONUNCIATION: hell-e-BORE-us ar-gew-ti-FOE-lee-us

COMMON NAME: Corsican hellebore

HOMELAND: Corsica

HARDINESS: USDA Zones 7–9

SIZE: 18″–24″ tall; up to 36″ across

INTEREST: Heavy clusters of pale green, cupped flowers remain handsome even after the petals have dropped. Evergreen, coarse, blue-green compound leaves, each leaflet armed and toothed along the margins. Flowers late winter to late spring.

LIGHT CONDITIONS: Light to moderate shade

SOIL/MOISTURE: Highly organic, well-drained soil, enriched with compost or leaf mold

DESCRIPTION: A bold accent plant in light woodlands; underplant with sweet woodruff or interplant with delicate ferns. In mixed or perennial borders, Corsican hellebore is a fine companion for astilbes, ligularias, corydalis, or hostas. Variegated lungworts and even pachysandra are attractive underplantings that accentuate the apple green flowers.

HEMEROCALLIS × *HYBRIDA*

PRONUNCIATION: hem-er-o-KAL-is × HIB-rid-a

COMMON NAME: Daylily

HOMELAND: Of garden origin

HARDINESS: USDA Zones 3–10

SIZE: 1′–4′ tall; 2′–3′ across

INTEREST: Bold clumps of grassy foliage. Funnel-shaped blossoms, 2″–5″ across and often ruffled, in yellows through melon shades to deepest red and mahogany. Flowers late spring to late summer by variety—most blooming for 3 to 4 weeks.

LIGHT CONDITIONS: Full sun to light shade

SOIL/MOISTURE: Well-drained, fertile or average soil is best, but tolerant of most soils.

DESCRIPTION: Although individual flowers last but a day, each scape (naked flower stem) carries several buds, which open in succession. The innumerable hybrids bloom over a long period, and catalogs list them as early, midseason, and late bloomers; some repeat-bloom. Extremely adaptable, daylilies are particularly appealing massed in open island beds or under the light dappled shade of small-leaved deciduous trees. Excellent in controlling erosion on exposed sunny banks; plant as a ground cover.

Hosta sieboldiana 'Elegans'
(plantain lily, funkia)

Liatris spicata (dense blazing
star, spike gayfeather)

Lysimachia ciliata
(fringed loosestrife)

LEFT
Iris versicolor
(blue iris, blue flag)

Hosta sieboldiana 'Elegans'

PRONUNCIATION: HOS-ta see-bol-dee-AY-na
COMMON NAME: Plantain lily, funkia
HOMELAND: Species from Japan; cultivar of garden origin
HARDINESS: USDA Zones 3–9
SIZE: 30″–36″ tall; up to 4′ across
INTEREST: Very pale lavender, almost white blossoms. Bold clumps of large cupped and puckered blue-gray leaves. Flowers mid-summer.
LIGHT CONDITIONS: Partial, dappled, or filtered light
SOIL/MOISTURE: Well-drained but moisture-retentive, organic soil

DESCRIPTION: This dramatic plant may be used as a high-profile specimen, perhaps accenting a magnificent outcropping or serving as a punctuation point where shady paths intersect; also beautiful in a container. In cloudy climes, contrast with blue oat grass, or maybe Japanese painted fern. Beware of slug and deer damage to emerging foliage, and remove damaged leaves if possible. Among the hostas, however, this one with "good substance" or thick leaves, is more slug-resistant than most.

Iris versicolor

PRONUNCIATION: EYE-ris VER-si-co-lor
COMMON NAME: Blue iris, blue flag
HOMELAND: Eastern Canada to Pennsylvania
HARDINESS: USDA Zones 3–8
SIZE: 2′–3′ tall; 12″–15″ across
INTEREST: In early to midsummer, fleeting blue to violet flowers, blotched with yellow and veined purple on the lower petals (falls), rise above a fan of broadly linear leaves.
LIGHT CONDITIONS: Light to dappled shade
SOIL/MOISTURE: Moist soil, of average fertility, that does not dry out. Wet meadows, bogs, or shallow standing water is ideal.

DESCRIPTION: Blue flags are attractive massed at water's edge, perhaps accented with an equal stand of yellow flags close by, or as a companion for cattails or cinnamon or royal ferns. The succulent roots may be devastated by muskrats and other water wildlife. Take care in handling the rootstock, as it can cause dermatitis on sensitive skin.

LIATRIS SPICATA

PRONUNCIATION: lee-AT-ris spi-KAH-ta
COMMON NAME: Dense blazing star, spike gayfeather
HOMELAND: Native; eastern and central United States, west to Louisiana
HARDINESS: USDA Zones 3–9
SIZE: 2'–4' tall; 18"–24" across

INTEREST: Dense bottlebrush spikes of fluffy magenta blossoms on erect leafy stems. Flowers mid- to late summer.
LIGHT CONDITIONS: Full sun to very light shade
SOIL/MOISTURE: Well-drained, fertile soil

DESCRIPTION: The strident color of this wildflower makes it difficult to incorporate into garden designs. It is probably best as an accent plant, rather than grouped in the border, but is quite at home in native-plant and wild gardens. The flowers open from the top down, making it long lasting as a cut flower. 'Kobold' is a compact 18" cultivar, with spikes reminiscent of Indian clubs; 'Floristan White' grows 2'–3' tall and bears creamy white flowers. *L. pycnostachya* is a prairie plant that should find its way into more gardens.

LYSIMACHIA CILIATA

PRONUNCIATION: lie-sim-AK-i-a skil-ee-AH-ta
COMMON NAME: Fringed loosestrife
HOMELAND: Quebec to British Columbia, south to Florida, Texas, and Arizona
HARDINESS: USDA Zones 3–9
SIZE: 1'–4' tall; about 2' across

INTEREST: Slender clumps with willowlike leaves, fringed with hairs. Light yellow 1" flowers in the upper leaf axils in mid- to late summer.
LIGHT CONDITIONS: Partial shade
SOIL/MOISTURE: Moist soil of average fertility

DESCRIPTION: Group at watersides and in other damp places, where their upright habit will contrast with bolder rounded shapes such as oak-leaved hydrangea and darmera. Not as invasive as some other loosestrifes, but be aware of its roving tendencies. 'Purpurea' has deep purplish black young growth; 'Atropurpurea' has bronze-red leaves.

Monarda didyma
(bee balm, Oswego tea,
bergamot)

Osmunda cinnamomea
(cinnamon fern)

Perovskia atriplicifolia
(Russian sage)

RIGHT
Paeonia lactiflora
'Krinkled White'
(common garden peony)

MONARDA DIDYMA

PRONUNCIATION: mon-AR-da DID-i-ma

COMMON NAME: Bee balm, Oswego tea, bergamot

HOMELAND: Native; New York to Michigan and south to Georgia and Tennessee

HARDINESS: USDA Zones 4–9

SIZE: 30"–48" tall; spreading to 4' across

INTEREST: Leafy clumps of square erect stems, with terminal clusters of bright red, 2-lipped flowers in mid-summer

LIGHT CONDITIONS: Light shade, especially in the South

SOIL/MOISTURE: Moisture-retentive, fertile soil

DESCRIPTION: A favorite in American herb and cottage gardens, bee balm is equally suitable in damp meadows. In the flower border, it is sometimes difficult to tame, as the underground stems spread rapidly. Many cultivars are available, some possibly hybrids with long-blooming, disease-resistant *M. fistulosa:* 'Cambridge Scarlet' and 'Gardenview Scarlet' are popular reds; 'Mahogany' has maroon-purple flowers; tall 'Blue Stocking' is a strong purple; and 'Croftway Pink' and 'Marshall's Delight' are pinks. Except for 'Gardenview Scarlet' and 'Marshall's Delight', mildew is a serious problem, especially when stressed by drought. Visited by hummingbirds, butterflies, and bees.

OSMUNDA CINNAMOMEA

PRONUNCIATION: oz-MUN-da sin-am-OHM-ee-a

COMMON NAME: Cinnamon fern

HOMELAND: Throughout North America to Mexico

HARDINESS: USDA Zones 2–10

SIZE: 30"–60" tall; 18"–30" across

INTEREST: Elegant, light green, deeply cut fronds. Fertile cinnamon-colored fronds, which die as soon as the spores are shed. Fertile fronds appear in late spring.

LIGHT CONDITIONS: Partial to light shade

SOIL/MOISTURE: Moisture-retentive, fertile soil, preferably acid

DESCRIPTION: This attractive deciduous fern does well in open or lightly shaded boggy or damp places. Excellent massed alone or with other ferns, or accompanied by hostas, daylilies, astilbes, primulas, and bergenias at streamside. Attractive under rhododendrons and mountain laurel for foliage contrast.

PAEONIA LACTIFLORA 'KRINKLED WHITE'

PRONUNCIATION: pay-OH-nee-a lak-ti-FLOR-a
COMMON NAME: Common garden peony
HOMELAND: Northeastern Asia; cultivar of garden origin
HARDINESS: USDA Zones 2–9
SIZE: 18"–42" tall; 2'–3' across
INTEREST: Substantial bushes of dark green, fingered leaves on long stems. Cultivars with single, double, or semidouble flowers in all colors except blue are available.
LIGHT CONDITIONS: Full sun to light shade
SOIL/MOISTURE: Moisture-retentive but well-drained, rich soil, amended with manure, compost, or leaf mold

DESCRIPTION: Peonies are one of the all-time favorite garden plants for their ease of culture and enormous variety. The handsome foliage remains in good condition throughout the season and makes a solid dark background for brightly colored annuals and perennials. Some cultivars have fall color. 'Krinkled White' has single white blooms. Others include 'Festiva Maxima', an early, double white flecked with crimson; 'Sarah Bernhardt', a late with rose-pink fragrant flowers; 'Scarlet O'Hara', a single red; and 'Kansas', an early, double deep red. Excellent for cutting. Double-flowered varieties need staking.

PEROVSKIA ATRIPLICIFOLIA

PRONUNCIATION: per-ROF-skee-a a-tri-plis-i-FOE-lee-a
COMMON NAME: Russian sage
HOMELAND: Western Pakistan
HARDINESS: USDA Zones 4–9
SIZE: 3'–5' tall; 2'–4' across
INTEREST: Small silvery gray leaves on stiff shrubby stems. Airy sprays of tiny blue or lavender flowers in mid- to late summer.
LIGHT CONDITIONS: Full sun
SOIL/MOISTURE: Very well drained soil of average fertility

DESCRIPTION: Fragrant Russian sage makes a thin shrubby plant, useful for adding lightness to the flower border. It can be used as a scrim plant, softening bold colors of annuals or perennials behind. Attractive with white *Rosa* 'Seafoam' or asters. Underplant with *Aster* 'Purple Dome' or 'Hella Lacy' for a vibrant effect, or allow it to support the floppy stems of *Aster* × *frikartii.* Heat and drought resistant and attractive to butterflies.

Phlox paniculata
(garden phlox)

Rudbeckia fulgida var.
sullivantii 'Goldsturm'
(orange coneflower)

Solidago species
(goldenrod)

LEFT
Tradescantia × *andersoniana*
(spiderwort)

Phlox paniculata

PRONUNCIATION: FLOKS pan-ik-ew-LAH-ta

COMMON NAME: Garden phlox

HOMELAND: Native; New York to Georgia and Arkansas

HARDINESS: USDA Zones 4–9

SIZE: 2'–5' tall; 18"–30" across

INTEREST: Clumps of leafy stems, terminating in large clusters of fragrant wheel-shaped flowers, magenta in the species. Cultivars in all colors except pure blue and yellow are available.

LIGHT CONDITIONS: Full sun to very light shade

SOIL/MOISTURE: Deep, well-drained, rich soil, amended with compost or leaf mold

DESCRIPTION: Garden phlox is a traditional plant of cottage gardens. To minimize mildew, choose a position where air movement is good; avoid planting phlox next to walls or dense hedges. Cull out diseased varieties. Combine with verbascum, globe thistles, tall veronicas, or other upright flowers according to your color scheme. The innumerable cultivars include 'Bright Eyes', pink with a crimson eye; white 'Mt. Fuji'; salmon 'Sir John Falstaff'; deep violet 'The King'; and deep red 'Othello'.

Rudbeckia fulgida var. *sullivantii* 'Goldsturm'

PRONUNCIATION: rood-BEK-ee-a FUL-jid-a var. sul-iv-ANT-ee-eye

COMMON NAME: Orange coneflower

HOMELAND: Of garden origin

HARDINESS: USDA Zones 3–9

SIZE: 24"–30" tall; 18"–24" across

INTEREST: Bright golden daisies, 2"–4" across, centered with an almost black cone. Nearly nonstop bloom in summer.

LIGHT CONDITIONS: Full sun

SOIL/MOISTURE: Well-drained, fertile soil, amended with compost or leaf mold

DESCRIPTION: Vegetatively propagated plants of this wonderful selection of black-eyed Susan have a uniformity that is desirable for mass plantings. On a smaller garden scale, that may not be important, but nevertheless this is a great perennial for long-term color. Partner it with other hot-colored plants such as the brassy daylilies, Mexican sunflowers, marigolds, and purple-flowered sages, or cool it off with silvery artemisias, Russian sage, or sea oats. Water deeply in dry weather. Espresso-brown seed heads are ornamental into winter.

SOLIDAGO SPECIES

PRONUNCIATION: sol-id-AY-go
COMMON NAME: Goldenrod
HOMELAND: Mostly North American; cultivars of garden origin
HARDINESS: USDA Zones 3–9
SIZE: 6"–4' tall and 1'–3' across, depending on species or cultivar

INTEREST: Crowded inflorescences of tiny, brilliant yellow daisy flowers in mid-summer to fall by species
LIGHT CONDITIONS: Full sun to very light shade
SOIL/MOISTURE: Well-drained, rich to average soil

DESCRIPTION: This variable genus, long admired in European gardens, is finally gaining respectability in this country. These include 2'–3'-tall 'Peter Pan'; 'Crown of Rays', at 2'; 18" 'Golden Fleece'; and 'Golden Thumb' and 'Gold Dwarf', both about 1' tall. Recently introduced *S. rugosa* 'Fireworks' is aptly named, as it has flower heads that appear to have exploded. All are excellent companions for asters. The species are appropriate for native and meadow gardens, but they are colonizers and may take over. All attract bees and butterflies.

TRADESCANTIA × *ANDERSONIANA*

PRONUNCIATION: tra-des-KANT-ee-a × an-der-son-ee-AYE-na
COMMON NAME: Spiderwort
HOMELAND: Of garden origin
HARDINESS: USDA Zones 5–10
SIZE: 1'–2' tall; 15"–18" across
INTEREST: Numerous 3-petaled flowers in late

spring. Bloom intermittently through the season. Although each blossom lasts but a day, their large number ensures bloom for several weeks.
LIGHT CONDITIONS: Sun to light shade
SOIL/MOISTURE: Well-drained soil of average fertility

DESCRIPTION: The hybrid spiderworts are popular cottage garden and border plants, and are best used as fillers, where their rather ungainly habit is not overly obvious. Divide or replace every 2 or 3 years to maintain vigor and curb excessive spreading. Cut back by half after the first flush of bloom when the foliage becomes shabby. Among the best known white cultivars are 'Osprey', which is accented with bright blue feathery stamens, and creamy white 'Innocence'. 'Pauline' has orchid pink flowers; 'Red Cloud' is a rosier red. 'Zwanenburg' has violet-purple flowers; those of 'Blue Stone' are medium blue.

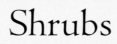

Shrubs

Shrubs

Often, the structure of a garden is referred to as its bones. In winter, the bones are revealed as walls, paths, the volume of evergreen shrubs, and the branch forms of deciduous ones. Shrubs make a great deal of the structure of a garden —they can be the living framework of the landscape.

Shrubs are traditionally used to solve problems, like hiding an unsightly view or a neighbor's idea of good outdoor taste. When I need a barrier, I love to make what I call a "bio-hedge" of plants like raspberries, landscape roses, and viburnums, which not only have flowers, but provide fruit, pollen, and nectar, as well as shelter for birds.

Shrubs work wonderfully to provide that all-important background foil for perennial borders. Broadleaf evergreens such as rhododendrons, *Pieris*, or *Pittosporum* will seem as solid as a wall—but are alive and flowering. But shrubs can be used within the perennial planting not only for their structure and mass, but for their flowers and the color and texture of their leaves. The smoke bushes, for example, come in shades from green to deep, velvety purple. All have frothy flowers.

Some shrubs are four-season plants. The oakleaf hydrangea has white flowers in early summer, which turn pink, then green, and finally a warm brown. In the fall, the leaves turn bronze-purple. Then the bark provides winter interest, tan and textured with papery exfoliating curls, like cinnamon sticks. Early in spring, the new growth comes—silver-green and lobed like oak leaves.

Think of the off-times in the garden when you select the shrubs. The witch hazels bloom very early, some in February. Forsythia is familiar to everyone; I like the ones with the palest yellow, which look less overpowering. Several evergreen viburnum bloom early, followed by star magnolias, early spireas, and the first lilacs.

As the gardening season ends, the shrubs may come back to the forefront with flowers, such as those on the rose-of-Sharon, *Hibiscus syriacus,* and the autumn-blooming witch hazel, *Hamamelis virginiana.* You may imagine it is all over come winter, but then some of the extraordinary tracery of twigs or stalwart trunks and bark of woody plants are revealed.

Ceanothus species
(California lilac)

Cotinus coggygria
(smokebush)

Euonymus alatus (winged
euonymus, burning bush)

LEFT
Hydrangea macrophylla
'Blue Wave' (blue wave
hydrangea, big-leaf
hydrangea, Lacecap
hydrangea)

CEANOTHUS SPECIES

PRONUNCIATION: see-an-OH-thus

COMMON NAME: California lilac

HOMELAND: Eastern United States, Rockies, Pacific Northwest, California, and Mexico

HARDINESS: USDA Zones 4–9

SIZE: Prostrate up to 20', depending on species

INTEREST: Often fragrant, white or blue, sometimes pink flowers in fluffy clusters in spring. Deciduous or evergreen shrubs or small trees.

LIGHT CONDITIONS: Full sun to shade

SOIL/MOISTURE: Very well drained, average soil, but on the light side

DESCRIPTION: Numerous ceanothus are on the market, most of which are hybrids. Among the species, the white-flowering New Jersey tea (*C. ovatus*) and its close cousin *C. americana* are hardy to Zone 4. In California and the West, the bright blue-flowered sorts are splendid. Many are cultivars of *C. gloriosus* and the *C.* × *delilianus* group. 'Anchor Bay' has very deep blue flowers on dense, spreading bushes 18" tall; taller *C. g. porrectus* bears paler flowers. 'Gloire de Versailles' has brilliant blue flowers; deer-resistant 'Dark Star' has dark cobalt blue flowers on a 6'-tall by 10'-wide shrub. *C. prostratus* makes an excellent ground cover.

COTINUS COGGYGRIA

PRONUNCIATION: ko-TIE-nus ko-GIG-ree-a

COMMON NAME: Smokebush

HOMELAND: Southern Europe to China, U.S.

HARDINESS: USDA Zones 4–9

SIZE: 15'–20' tall; 6'–8' or more across

INTEREST: Multistemmed shrub, clothed with oval 2"–3" leaves. Inconspicuous flower clusters are carried in large branching inflorescences, each branch covered with hairs, which change color as the season progresses. Brilliant fall color. Flowers mid- to late summer.

LIGHT CONDITIONS: Full sun to light shade. Varieties grown for leaf color are more vivid in sun.

SOIL/MOISTURE: Well-drained soil, but tolerant of a wide range

DESCRIPTION: Grown for the interesting "smoke" effect, smokebush puts on its best display from early summer to early fall. It is more effective in a collection of shrubs than as a specimen, as its habit is often ungainly. Purple-leaved forms are popular for their interesting foliage as well as for the purplish "smoke"; 'Royal Purple' and 'Velvet Cloak' both grow about 8' tall. These are often "coppiced" (cut to the ground) in early spring to encourage young, more colorful growth, but this eliminates the puffy smoke effect. Contrast with silver-leaved thistles, artichokes, or Russian sage.

EUONYMUS ALATUS

PRONUNCIATION: yew-ON-i-mus a-LAY-tus

COMMON NAME: Winged euonymus, burning bush

HOMELAND: Northeast Asia to mid-China

HARDINESS: USDA Zones 4–9

SIZE: Up to 20' tall and as wide

INTEREST: Stems and twigs adorned with flat, corky wings for winter interest. Pest-free foliage that turns brilliant deep red in fall.

LIGHT CONDITIONS: Full sun to shade

SOIL/MOISTURE: Tolerates a wide range of soils, but not wet feet.

DESCRIPTION: Winged euonymus is such a forgiving bush and performs with such little care that it has become badly overused. It makes a fine hedge and takes clipping well; mass as a thick screen, or group in the open landscape or beside water. In a foundation planting it can be kept within bounds by clipping and provides good year-round contrast with junipers, arborvitae, or false cypress, especially when decked in its fall finery. Several selections are on the market. Full-size 'Compactus' has less pronounced wings on the stems but finer winter texture; 'Monstrosa' has bold corky ridges on the stems. 'Nordine' is more compact than the species and has branches low to the ground.

HYDRANGEA MACROPHYLLA 'BLUE WAVE'

PRONUNCIATION: hi-DRAN-jee-a mak-ro-FIL-la

COMMON NAME: Blue wave hydrangea, big-leaf hydrangea, Lacecap hydrangea

HOMELAND: Japan, cultivar of garden origin

HARDINESS: USDA Zones 6–8

SIZE: 5' tall or more; 4'–6' across

INTEREST: 6" wide, flat flowers in round clusters form at the ends of 1-and 2-year-old stems. This cultivar (perhaps a hybrid) has flat, sterile blossoms surrounding fertile beadlike ones in mid-summer.

LIGHT CONDITIONS: Full sun to light shade

SOIL/MOISTURE: Well-drained but moisture-retentive soil

DESCRIPTION: Hydrangeas are among the most beloved of all shrubs. The large-leafed types are probably the most familiar with their mop-head flower clusters forming nearly complete balls. Varieties may be pink, red, or white, but most often blue. Many varieties react to acid in the soil—becoming bluer the more acidic the soil is, and pink in alkaline soil. 'Nikko Blue' is a vigorous variety. Not plagued by pests, the tender flower and leaf buds are most frequently killed by the cold of winter. Prune out woody canes at the ground, which will not flower. No other pruning is necessary, except to remove winter-damaged growth.

Forsythia × *intermedia*
(border forsythia)

Hamamelis × *intermedia*
'Jelena' (copper
witch hazel)

Hibiscus syriacus 'Bluebird'
(rose-of-Sharon,
shrub althea)

Lavandula angustifolia
(English lavender)

FORSYTHIA × INTERMEDIA

PRONUNCIATION: for-SITH-ee-a × in-ter-
MEE-dee-a

COMMON NAME: Border forsythia

HOMELAND: Of garden origin

HARDINESS: USDA Zones 5–9

SIZE: 8'–10' tall and as wide or wider

INTEREST: Coarse, rangy deciduous shrub with cheerfully seductive, brilliant yellow flowers in late winter.

LIGHT CONDITIONS: Full sun to light shade (will grow in deeper shade as foliage plant without flowers)

SOIL/MOISTURE: Tolerates almost any soil but not wet feet.

DESCRIPTION: This harbinger of spring, especially in cold regions, brings little interest to the garden outside of its bloom time. Plant as part of a shrub collection, or allow it to spread at will in a wild or transitional part of the garden. Useful massed on difficult banks. Prune out old wood or prune drastically to the ground after blooming; the best flowers are on young wood. Never shear; a large part of the charm of forsythia is its exuberant growth (and a bright yellow bowling ball would not look right with the natural garden).

HAMAMELIS × INTERMEDIA 'JELENA'

PRONUNCIATION: ham-a-MEE-lis × in-ter-
MEE-dee-a

COMMON NAME: Copper witch hazel

HOMELAND: Of garden origin

HARDINESS: USDA Zones 5–8

SIZE: 15'–20' tall; 6'–10' across

INTEREST: This large, open vase-shaped shrub bears oval leaves that turn red, bronze, and orange in fall. The fragrant blossoms have a coppery glow; the curling, spidery petals are orange at the base and yellow at the tips. Flowers late winter to early spring.

LIGHT CONDITIONS: Full sun to partial shade

SOIL/MOISTURE: Moisture-retentive, acid soil, enriched with plenty of organic material

DESCRIPTION: Belgian-bred 'Jelena' is one of the best of the copper-flowered witch hazel cultivars. Site it so that it is backlit by the rising or setting sun. Best used as a specimen, since its unique characteristics are lost in a shrub collection. Underplant with early-flowering species crocus, snowdrops, and winter aconites. Other reliable cultivars include long-blooming, rich yellow-flowered 'Arnold Promise'; primrose-yellow 'Westerstede', red-flowered 'Diana', which also has good fall color; and 10'-tall 'Firecracker', which can be trained as an espalier or on a fence.

HIBISCUS SYRIACUS 'BLUEBIRD'

PRONUNCIATION: hi-BIS-kus si-ri-A-kus
COMMON NAME: Rose-of-Sharon, shrub althea
HOMELAND: China and India; cultivar of garden origin
HARDINESS: USDA Zones 5—8
SIZE: 8'—12' tall; 6'—10' across
INTEREST: Handsome lobed foliage on erect or spreading, single or multistemmed plants. Violet-blue, 3½" bowl-shaped flowers, accented with a maroon eye in late summer into fall.
LIGHT CONDITIONS: Full sun to partial shade
SOIL/MOISTURE: Moist, organic soil that drains well

DESCRIPTION: Perhaps still the best single blue, this old cultivar may have been grown 100 years or more ago. Can be pruned up as a small tree or trained more as a large bush; flowers are borne on the current season's wood. Tolerant of seaside conditions. Partner 'Bluebird' with a purple-leaved smokebush cultivar, which will pick up the maroon eye color of the flowers. Other good cultivars include dark pink 'Aphrodite' and pure white 'Diana', which forms fewer fruits and therefore blooms longer with larger flowers. Double-flowered varieties are also available.

LAVANDULA ANGUSTIFOLIA

PRONUNCIATION: la-VAN-dew-la an-gust-i-FOL-ee-a
COMMON NAME: English lavender
HOMELAND: Mediterranean region
HARDINESS: USDA Zones 5—9
SIZE: 1'—3' tall and as wide
INTEREST: Fragrant, grayish blue-green, needlelike leaves. The spikes of lavender-blue flowers bloom in summer.
LIGHT CONDITIONS: Full sun
SOIL/MOISTURE: Well-drained, dryish soil. Add lime to acid soils.

DESCRIPTION: Long planted in herb, fragrance, and cottage gardens, lavender is also useful in other parts of the garden. It tolerates shearing (what a pleasurable task!) and makes a fine clipped hedge. Its foliage texture contrasts well with dark rhododendrons or even roses. Several cultivars are available: 'Munstead' has large blue-lilac flowers to 18" tall; 'Hidcote' is more compact, but the spent flower spikes hold their color well. 'Jean Davis' is a pink-flowered cultivar; 'Lavender Lady' blooms the first year from seed. Trim shabby growth as soon as new shoots break in spring.

Lindera angustifolia
(Asian spicebush)

Magnolia stellata
(star magnolia)

Pittosporum tobira
'Variegatum' (variegated
Japanese pittosporum)

LEFT
Pieris japonica
'Variegata' (variegated
Japanese pieris, variegated
Japanese andromeda)

LINDERA ANGUSTIFOLIA

PRONUNCIATION: lin-DARE-a an-gus-ti-FO-lia
COMMON NAME: Asian spicebush
HOMELAND: East Asia
HARDINESS: USDA Zones 6–8
SIZE: 10'–12' or more tall and almost as wide
INTEREST: Vase-shaped shrub has smooth gray bark and pest-free lanceolate leaves that turn orange-scarlet, then apricot in fall, contrasting well with blue-black berries. These persist through the winter, soft tan in color.
LIGHT CONDITIONS: Full sun or very light shade
SOIL/MOISTURE: Average soil, with good drainage

DESCRIPTION: This Asiatic spicebush is a welcome addition to the inventory of shrubs for American gardens, but is currently hard to find in the marketplace. A striking winter backdrop for the white-bloomed stems of *Salix irrorata* and brilliant scarlet winter stems of *S. alba* 'Chermesena'. Superb cut at the height of its fall color or later in its apricot-cinnamon dress as a long-lasting, dried branch. In damp woods of the northeast, native spicebush *L. benzoin* blooms in early spring, with fluffy yellow flowers. It may reach 12' or so and is best planted in a shrub collection, either in sun or light shade. Lovely yellow fall color, but the leaves drop before winter.

MAGNOLIA STELLATA

PRONUNCIATION: mag-NO-lee-a ste-LA-ta
COMMON NAME: Star magnolia
HOMELAND: Japan
HARDINESS: USDA Zones 4–8
SIZE: 15'–20' tall; to 15' or so wide
INTEREST: Stocky tree or shrub with fine gray bark and furry winter buds. Fragrant flowers with 12–18 pure white, strap-shaped petals appear in early to mid-spring, before the leaves emerge. Yellow fall color.
LIGHT CONDITIONS: Full sun to very light shade
SOIL/MOISTURE: Deep, moist, acid soil, amended with compost or leaf mold

DESCRIPTION: Star magnolia blooms ahead of the saucer magnolia but is also susceptible to frost damage at blooming time. In the North do not plant with a southern exposure that hastens flower opening. Provide a dark background of rhododendrons, hemlocks, or other evergreens to show off the pristine flowers on the ends of smooth, gray barked branches. Many-petaled 'Royal Star' has pink buds that open to 3"–4" pure white flowers, 'Centennial' also bears many petals blushed with pink. 'Waterlily' has fine fragrance.

PIERIS JAPONICA 'VARIEGATA'

PRONUNCIATION: pi-AIR-is ja-PON-ik-a

COMMON NAME: Variegated Japanese pieris, variegated Japanese andromeda

HOMELAND: Japan; cultivar of garden origin

HARDINESS: USDA Zones 5–8

SIZE: 10'–12' tall; 6'–8' across

INTEREST: Beautiful evergreen foliage, dark green, edged with clean white. Drooping clusters of cream lily-of-the-valley flowers in spring; winter flower buds are also interesting.

LIGHT CONDITIONS: Light dappled shade to open woodland

SOIL/MOISTURE: Well-drained, fertile soil, amended with leaf mold or compost

DESCRIPTION: Japanese pieris is a superior shrub, but in its variegated form it is superb. It grows fairly slowly and fits into small residential gardens with ease. Use as a specimen plant, perhaps in the ell of a building or as a focal point for a group of shrubs. It also tolerates container culture, and can dress up a terrace or rooftop for the whole year. Shelter from the wind and be alert for lace bug damage. There are numerous other cultivars of the species.

PITTOSPORUM TOBIRA 'VARIEGATUM'

PRONUNCIATION: pit-o-SPO-rum to-BY-ra

COMMON NAME: Variegated Japanese pittosporum

HOMELAND: Japan, China, and Korea; cultivar of garden origin

HARDINESS: USDA Zones 9–10

SIZE: 10'–12' tall; half again as wide

INTEREST: Slow-growing, dense evergreen shrub with gray-green foliage irregularly edged with white. Small, very fragrant flowers in 2"–3"-wide clusters, popcorn-white blossoms age to yellow. Flowers in spring.

LIGHT CONDITIONS: Full sun to shade

SOIL/MOISTURE: Tolerates a wide range of soils, as long as the soil is well drained.

DESCRIPTION: In warm climates, pittosporum is used in foundation plantings and mass plantings and is clipped for hedges or screens. Elsewhere it is a popular container plant for sunrooms and greenhouses, often grown with brilliantly colored bougainvilleas. The green-and-white foliage of 'Variegata' makes it especially handsome. 'Wheeler's Dwarf' is a 1'–2' compact form with lustrous, all-green foliage.

Rhus typhina 'Laciniata'
(cutleaf staghorn sumac)

Rosa 'Carefree Beauty'
(rose)

Rubus idaeus 'Heritage'
(everblooming raspberry)

RIGHT
Rhododendron hybrids and
cultivars (rhododendron)

RHODODENDRON HYBRIDS AND CULTIVARS

PRONUNCIATION: roe-doe-DEN-dron

COMMON NAME: Rhododendron

HOMELAND: China, Japan, and North America; hybrids and cultivars of garden origin

HARDINESS: USDA Zones 5–8

SIZE: 1'–12' tall and 3'–10' across, depending on parentage

INTEREST: Glossy, evergreen foliage, often covered with tan hairs (indumentum) on the undersides, which feel like suede. Delicate or waxy, bell-shaped blossoms in all colors except true blue, mostly in spring.

LIGHT CONDITIONS: Light to medium shade

SOIL/MOISTURE: Organic soil, with compost or leaf mold

DESCRIPTION: One of the largest groups of ornamental shrubs, rhododendrons and azaleas are botanically the same genus, but in the vernacular they are often divided: the former being large-leaved evergreen, the latter twiggy and deciduous. As understory shrubs, rhododendrons are without peer. Try any of the Kurumes, Catawbiense, or Maximum hybrids, and mass them in light woodland. The Indica hybrids and "Gable" hybrids are also widespread. Prune only dead or damaged wood and remove spent flower trusses, to concentrate the plant's energy on the formation of next year's flower buds rather than on seed production.

RHUS TYPHINA

PRONUNCIATION: ROOSE ty-FY-na

COMMON NAME: Cutleaf staghorn sumac

HOMELAND: Southeastern Canada, south to Georgia, Indiana, and Iowa; cultivar of garden origin

HARDINESS: USDA Zones 3–8

SIZE: 15'–25' tall and as wide from suckers

INTEREST: Deciduous, deeply cut leaves, which turn brilliant shades of yellow, orange, and red in fall. New growth densely covered with soft hairs. Rusty crimson, fuzzy fruit clusters in fall.

LIGHT CONDITIONS: Full sun

SOIL/MOISTURE: Well-drained, average soil. Tolerates dry, poor soils well.

DESCRIPTION: The species is often found in the wild along rough dry roadsides and railroad tracks and is suitable for large naturalistic settings. The fernleaf sumac may be used as a huge specimen plant, perhaps in the open as a focal point, or, if space allows, in the ell of a building, where in winter its interesting branching pattern can be seen. In cold areas, or as the short-lived plants age, suckers produce new shoots—a blessing or a curse depending on their chosen place in the landscape.

ROSA 'CAREFREE BEAUTY'

PRONUNCIATION: ROE-sa
COMMON NAME: Rose
HOMELAND: Of garden origin
HARDINESS: USDA Zones 4–9
SIZE: 4'–5' tall; 3' or so wide
INTEREST: This vigorous shrub has medium pink, loosely double flowers that first flush in early summer, then bloom intermittently, and often produce a mini-flush when the weather cools in fall. Orange hips follow first flowers.
LIGHT CONDITIONS: Full sun
SOIL/MOISTURE: Rich, well-drained soil

DESCRIPTION: 'Carefree Beauty' is a hybrid shrub rose, best massed or planted close as a hedge. It also makes a good specimen plant. Underplant with lavender, catmint, clove pinks, or calamint for fragrance. Prune out old canes in late winter, thin weak canes, and cut back strong ones by a third. Resistant to black spot, mildew, and rust. This plant is one of several easy-to-grow introductions called "landscape roses." Others include: 'Carefree Wonder', 'Bonica', 'Simplicity', and low-growing 'The Fairy'.

RUBUS IDAEUS 'HERITAGE'

PRONUNCIATION: ROO-bus eye-DAY-ee-us
COMMON NAME: Everblooming raspberry
HOMELAND: Northern Europe, Asia, and North America; cultivar of garden origin
HARDINESS: USDA Zones 4–8
SIZE: 3'–4' tall; suckering to 3' across
INTEREST: Delicious red fruit in summer and a second late summer to fall crop
LIGHT CONDITIONS: Full sun to light shade
SOIL/MOISTURE: Very rich, moisture-retentive soil

DESCRIPTION: Raspberry fruits must be one of the delights of a home garden for food, but they also fit into the natural garden with ease. Plant as a hedge or barrier, and prune the spent canes out annually or allow them to naturalize in exuberant fashion. Look for certified virus-free stock from a reliable nursery that specializes in fruit. 'Heritage' is the best everbearing red raspberry on the market. Everbearing 'Fall Gold', with beautiful yellow fruits, has, like 'Heritage', few thorns and presents easy-to-pick fruits on the tips of the canes. Cut out the canes of repeat-bearers after their second, late-season crop.

Spiraea × *vanhouttei*
(Vanhoutte spirea,
Vanhoutte bridal wreath)

Viburnum opulus (highbush
cranberry, European
cranberry bush)

Weigela florida
(old-fashioned weigela)

LEFT
Syringa vulgaris
(common lilac)

SPIRAEA × VANHOUTTEI

PRONUNCIATION: spy-REE-a × van-HOOT-ee-eye

COMMON NAME: Vanhoutte spirea, Vanhoutte bridal wreath

HOMELAND: Of garden origin

HARDINESS: USDA Zones 3–7

SIZE: 6'–8' tall; 10'–12' across

INTEREST: Fountain-shaped shrub with arching branches profusely covered with small white flowers in spring

LIGHT CONDITIONS: Full sun to partial shade

SOIL/MOISTURE: Well-drained, average soil

DESCRIPTION: Although too large for many modern gardens, Vanhoutte spirea is still widely grown. Plant in a shrub collection or to back a mixed or perennial border. It also makes a good informal screen or hedge. After flowering, prune out older stems to the ground annually to shape. No fall color or fruits. Underplant with hyacinths, tulips, or daffodils for a spring display. S. × bumalda, 3' tall and wide, and its cultivar 'Goldflame' have pink flowers. The latter is prized for its bright yellow foliage, attractive with yellow roses and yellow lilies. Many other spireas and their hybrid forms are on the market.

SYRINGA VULGARIS

PRONUNCIATION: si-RING-ga vul-GAR-is

COMMON NAME: Common lilac

HOMELAND: Southern Europe

HARDINESS: USDA Zones 3–8

SIZE: 8'–15' or more tall; spreading to 6'–10' across

INTEREST: Deciduous shrub bearing large trusses of fragrant lilac-colored flowers in mid- to late spring

LIGHT CONDITIONS: Full sun to very light shade

SOIL/MOISTURE: Tolerant of a wide range of soil conditions

DESCRIPTION: These plants are beloved for their wonderful scent that evokes memories of a simpler time. There are countless cultivars in white, blue, lavender, purple, violet, pink, and magenta. Some have better fragrance than others. 'Krasavitska Moskvy' has fragrant, double flowers, rosy in the bud, opening white; 'Sensation' is reddish violet, each flower outlined in white. 'President Lincoln' is the bluest of all, but grows tall—presenting fragrant blossoms for the second-story window. Other cultivars, species, and hybrids are more in scale with small urban gardens. Plant as a hedge, barrier, or in a shrub collection where summer humidity is low to avoid mildew. (Photo with 'Lady Bank's' rose.)

VIBURNUM OPULUS

PRONUNCIATION: vy-BER-num OP-yew-lus

COMMON NAME: Highbush cranberry, European cranberry bush

HOMELAND: Europe, northern Africa, and northern Asia

HARDINESS: USDA Zones 3–8

SIZE: 8'–10' tall; up to 10' or more wide

INTEREST: An upright, multistemmed, deciduous shrub bearing glossy foliage in summer, which turns yellow or reddish in fall. The flat-topped clusters of white blossoms, showy and sterile around the edge, tiny and fertile within, result in persistent bright red, round fruits in fall. Flowers in late-spring to early summer.

LIGHT CONDITIONS: Full sun to partial shade

SOIL/MOISTURE: Tolerant of a wide range of soils

DESCRIPTION: Highbush cranberry is best planted as a screen, or massed in large areas. It combines well with other shrubs but may not be sufficiently refined to plant as a specimen. 'Compactum' tops out at 4'–5' and is a better choice where space is limited. 'Nanum' is a dense, dwarf form, mostly non-flowering and nonfruiting, but useful as a filler plant. 'Xanthocarpum' is a yellow-fruited form. 'Roseum' ['Sterile'] is the familiar "snowball bush."

WEIGELA FLORIDA

PRONUNCIATION: wy-GE-la FLOR-i-da

COMMON NAME: Old-fashioned weigela

HOMELAND: Japan

HARDINESS: USDA Zones 4–9

SIZE: 6'–9' tall; 8'–9' across

INTEREST: Dense, rounded deciduous shrub with arching outer branches. Rosy pink, funnel-shaped flowers in early summer. No fragrance or fall color.

LIGHT CONDITIONS: Full sun

SOIL/MOISTURE: Well-drained, rich to average soil

DESCRIPTION: Although beautiful during its short blooming time, weigela is large and best mixed with other shrubs in collections, or behind perennials or smaller shrubs in the border. Prune flowered wood to the ground after second year bloom, and keep dead wood removed. The numerous cultivars and hybrids include white-flowered 'Candida', and 'Red Prince', with red flowers that attract hummingbirds. Red-flowered 'Tango' is a 2'-tall dwarf with fine wine-colored foliage. 'Java Red' also has red leaves; those of 'Variegata' are rimmed with cream or white; 'Rubidor' has gold foliage and red flowers.

Vines

Vines

Vines can share characteristics of many other plants in this book: there are annual vines, woody vines (somewhat like elongated shrubs), and ones that are herbaceous. What makes vines unique is that they climb. Vines fill the space from the shrubs up to the trees and above—another layer in the hierarchy of nature's design.

The ways the vines get from here to up there are varied and fascinating. Some twine. A twirling stem tip will search space for a physical means of support. When it comes in contact with its target, it starts to twine. The way this works is that cells on one side of the stem begin to divide at a much faster rate than those on the other side and the stem spirals around the support. Morning glories and wisteria are two examples. Interestingly, Japanese wisteria twines clockwise and Chinese wisteria twines counterclockwise. If you try to encourage a vine to attach to a support by winding it, it will often fall off, especially if you wrap it in the direction opposite from the way it grows in nature.

Some other vines have tendrils or hold-fasts. Tendrils are modified leaf stems that twist around a structure. Some of these, such as the passionflower's, also spiral along their length to create springs that act as reinforcing shock-absorbers, helping the plant sustain the weight of its top growth and resist wind. Clematis takes the tendril-leaf-stem morphology to a simpler step: the stem of the leaf itself winds around a support. Hold-fasts have little disks at the ends of their modified leaf stems which look like little suction cups and attach to supports with a kind of glue. Boston ivy and Virginia creeper are two examples.

Other vines, like English ivy and its relatives (*Hedera* species and cultivars), have little aerial rootlets that grow toward a support and attach to it. Climbing hydrangea and its lesser-known but magnificent cousin, *Schizophragma*, also possess these. It is important to know this, because if you are trying to cover a wall, you need to choose a plant with rootlets or holdfasts. If you want annual morning glories in front of the wall, you will have to put up twine or fishing line. If a long-lived vine like wisteria is your choice for the wall, you will need a permanent support like a trellis.

Hedera helix 'Pedata'
(bird's-foot ivy)

Lonicera ✕ *heckrottii*
(everblooming or
goldflame honeysuckle)

Parthenocissus tricuspidata
(Boston ivy)

RIGHT
Clematis ✕ *jackmanii*
(Jackman clematis)

CLEMATIS × JACKMANII

PRONUNCIATION: KLEM-a-tis ×
jak-MAN-ee-eye
COMMON NAME: Jackman clematis
HOMELAND: Of garden origin
HARDINESS: USDA Zones 3–9
SIZE: Climbs 6' or up to 18' on a support; 2'
across
INTEREST: Fast-growing twining vine with
strong purple, wheel-shaped flowers, to 6"
across, in summer and intermittently through
the season
LIGHT CONDITIONS: Full sun in the North
but light shade elsewhere
SOIL/MOISTURE: Moist, rich soil, amended
with compost or leaf mold to keep the roots
cool. A dressing of lime may be beneficial.

DESCRIPTION: Jackman clematis was the first of the large-flowered hybrids, and since has spawned a whole group of *Jackmanii* hybrids in assorted colors. They are superb for scrambling up posts, trellises, fences, and arbors, and they make themselves quite at home sprawling over other shrubs and even evergreens. Accent *Rosa* 'New Dawn' with deep purple *C.* × *jackmanii.* The dark velvety ruby flowers of 'Niobe' are sensational with golden hop vine (*Humulus Lupulus* 'Aureus'); try shell pink 'Hagley Hybrid' on a dark yew or rhododendron. The combinations are endless.

HEDERA HELIX 'PEDATA'

PRONUNCIATION: HED-er-a HE-liks
COMMON NAME: Bird's-foot ivy
HOMELAND: Caucasus mountains; cultivar of
garden origin
HARDINESS: USDA Zones 4–9
SIZE: 6"–8" tall as a ground cover, but may
climb to 50' or more
INTEREST: Fine-textured, dark green, evergreen foliage shaped like a bird's foot. No
flowers.
LIGHT CONDITIONS: Light to deep shade;
protect from strong winter sun.
SOIL/MOISTURE: Average to damp, well-
drained soil with plenty of organic matter is
best, but tolerates drier conditions.

DESCRIPTION: A refined ground-cover plant. Underplant with spring-flowering small daffodils and narcissus, and with *Colchicum* or *Crocus speciosus* for a fall display. Highlight with *Liriope muscari* 'Variegata' or variegated hostas such as 'Antioch' or *Hosta undulata* var. *erromena;* or, in summer, allow *Vinca major* 'Variegata' to trail across it to lighten the scene.

LONICERA × HECKROTTII

PRONUNCIATION: lon-ISS-era × hek-ROT-ee-eye

COMMON NAME: Everblooming or goldflame honeysuckle

HOMELAND: Of garden origin

HARDINESS: USDA Zones 4–9

SIZE: 10'–20' tall; 2' wide

INTEREST: Carmine red flower buds that open to reveal butter yellow insides with a light fragrance. Pink stems and semievergreen, blue-green foliage. Flowers late spring to early summer and sporadically until fall frost.

LIGHT CONDITIONS: Light, partial, to dappled shade

SOIL/MOISTURE: Soil of rich to average fertility that does not dry out excessively

DESCRIPTION: One of the best climbers of the genus, goldflame honeysuckle blooms from late spring right through until fall. Furnish it with an arch, trellis, pergola, or stainless-steel wire on which to climb and show off its beautiful foliage and flowers, preferably close to a sitting area where it and its light fragrance can be appreciated. But select a site with good air circulation, as this vine is prone to mildew. If aphids appear, wash them off with plain water in a spray from the garden hose. Can be grown as a mounded shrub if pruned routinely. Attractive to hummingbirds.

PARTHENOCISSUS TRICUSPIDATA

PRONUNCIATION: par-the-no-SIS-us tri-kus-pi-DA-ta

COMMON NAME: Boston ivy

HOMELAND: Japan and central China

HARDINESS: USDA Zones 4–8

SIZE: Up to 90' or more; 5'–10' wide

INTEREST: Deciduous 3-lobed leaves, to 8" across and shaped like a duck's foot, that turn bright yellow to bronzy black in fall. Semievergreen in mild climates. Magnificent florets.

LIGHT CONDITIONS: Full sun to partial shade

SOIL/MOISTURE: Tolerant of a wide range of soils, and even dry conditions once established

DESCRIPTION: One of the most popular climbing plants for covering buildings, pillars, and other stonework, especially under urban conditions, where it tolerates pollution well. This is the ivy of the "Ivy League." 'Lowii' has small frilly leaves; 'Veitchii' also has small leaves, which are purplish when young. 'Fenway Park' (discovered growing on a wall there) is a gold-leafed cultivar that will be on the market soon.

Passiflora vitifolia
(grapeleaf passionflower)

Polygonum aubertii
(silver lace vine)

Wisteria sinensis
(Chinese wiseteria)

Schisandra chinensis
(magnolia vine)

PASSIFLORA VITIFOLIA

PRONUNCIATION: pass-i-FLOR-a vit-i-FOE-lee-a

COMMON NAME: Grapeleaf passionflower

HOMELAND: Central and South America

HARDINESS: USDA Zones 10–11

SIZE: 6'–20' with a support; 2'–3' wide

INTEREST: Bright red, wheel-shaped blossoms—4" in diameter—among glossy, grayish green, tri-lobed leaves, on twining stems woolly with reddish hairs. Flowers spring, summer, and fall.

LIGHT CONDITIONS: Full sun to light shade

SOIL/MOISTURE: Well-drained, richly organic soil

DESCRIPTION: This tropical vine is used as a sunroom or greenhouse plant in cooler regions, where it is usually grown in a container. In subtropical zones, grapeleaf passionflower is planted to adorn trellises and arbors, and it can be used as an annual vine in northern gardens where summers are hot. In all cases, prune out old and weak stems in late winter. Bloom occurs on new growth. Egg-shaped, 2½" fruits follow.

POLYGONUM AUBERTII

PRONUNCIATION: poe-LIG-oh-num aw-BERT-ee-eye

COMMON NAME: Silver lace vine

HOMELAND: Western China

HARDINESS: USDA Zones 4–7

SIZE: Vining to 12'–35'; 2'–3' across

INTEREST: Great foamy oceans of slender sprays of greenish white or pinkish flowers in late summer and fall

LIGHT CONDITIONS: Full sun to shade

SOIL/MOISTURE: Tolerant of most soils, even dry ones

DESCRIPTION: This rampant vine rapidly swallows up chainlink fences and other unsightly structures, as well as adorning arbors and pergolas. Its foliage is good-looking all season long, and it is a valuable climber where little else will grow. Tolerates urban pollution well. Avoid unwanted seedlings by removing spent flower clusters. Prune hard to keep within bounds, and do not plant this vine in proximity to wild or wildlike areas, where it could become a pest.

SCHISANDRA CHINENSIS

PRONUNCIATION: sky-SAN-dra chi-NEN-sis
COMMON NAME: Magnolia vine
HOMELAND: Eastern Asia
HARDINESS: USDA Zones 6–9
SIZE: Up to 25'; 3'–5' wide
INTEREST: This woody deciduous vine has lustrous, toothed leaves to 4" long from dark pink leaf stems and, in spring, clusters of small, fragrant, creamy white translucent flowers. These are followed in fall by striking pendent clusters of scarlet fruits.
LIGHT CONDITIONS: Partial shade to shade
SOIL/MOISTURE: Well-drained, fertile soil that remains moist

DESCRIPTION: This twiner needs support on which to grow, or it can be allowed to scramble over rocks, walls, or tree stumps. Prune in late winter to contain excessive growth. Attractive when planted with yews or other dark evergreens, so that the berries are displayed to good advantage in fall. Parts of the vine will even grow in the dense shade within a year.

WISTERIA SINENSIS

PRONUNCIATION: wis-TEE-ree-a si-NEN-sis
COMMON NAME: Chinese wisteria
HOMELAND: China
HARDINESS: USDA Zones 4–9
SIZE: Climbs to 50'; 2'–3' across
INTEREST: A deciduous, counterclockwise climber with 6"–12"-long, drooping trusses of fragrant, lilac-blue pea flowers in late spring
LIGHT CONDITIONS: Full sun
SOIL/MOISTURE: Deep, well-drained soil that retains moisture in summer. Amend with compost or leaf mold.

DESCRIPTION: Chinese wisteria is very similar to the Japanese species, *Wisteria floribunda,* but the flower color is darker, and the Japanese vine's stems twine clockwise. Both grow rapidly to cover arbors, pergolas, fences, and other supports with no problem. Prune stems hard 2–4 weeks after flowering, to 3–5 buds, and continue to prune back through the season and in winter to promote thick, blooming spurs. If flowers are sparse, root-prune and avoid fertilizers high in nitrogen. Can be trained as a standard on a stout metal stake. Beware: This vine will twine under roof shingles and eventually pull down a clapboard house. There is a native species, but it is rarely offered by nurseries.

Bulbs

Bulbs

Flower bulbs are synonymous with spring. Daffodils ebb and flow under high-limbed birch trees and through areas of grass lawn that can be left unmown long enough for bulbs to ripen and foliage to yellow. Bulbs planted in drifts, as they would appear in nature, do much to naturalize a space. If the bulbs are shade-tolerant kinds, such as English bluebells, they might grow right under trees. Cluster species tulips, which have subtle colors and forms and are perennial, at the entrance to the woodland path or the edge of the herbaceous perennial planting. Try a small grouping of minor bulbs, which bloom early with tiny flowers, where they can't be missed, such as by the steps to the kitchen door: grape hyacinths or crocus, for example.

Imagine a planting of a rich, refined tulip selection such as 'Princess Irene', a cultivar with nearly indescribable colors

—petals of muted pumpkin overlaid with murky purple-brown streaks. These might be planted under the variegated grass *Phalaris arundinacea* 'Picta', or gardener's garters. The new shoots of the grass, emerging in spring, push up from the ground as 'Princess Irene' blooms, and when she has finished, they cover the spent blooms. Hostas and bulbs are also good companions, because most hostas sprout late, as spring bulbs complete their performance.

Remember that the bulb show is not limited to spring—lilies flower through summer, and *Colchicum* blossom in fall. Hardy cyclamen bloom in late summer and into fall. These plants are wonderful for that great gardening challenge—dry shade—and can be planted among deciduous ground covers or in the leaf litter that mulches the floor beneath the trees. Although they flower with exquisite little pink or white flared crowns on recurved stems, I love them for what follows the flowers as well. *Cyclamen hederifolium* flowers, for example, spring up from bare ground from August to November. Halfway through the blossoming season, the ivy-like leaves emerge. Often they are deep lagoon green, mottled or marbled, with overlays of silver or pewter. Be sure that these species bulbs, and all other species (as opposed to hybrids or cultivated varieties), are nursery propagated and not wild collected. The catalog should specify this.

Clivia miniata (clivia, Lady Clive's lily)

Erythronium tuolumnense (pagoda lily)

Fritillaria imperialis 'Lutea' (yellow crown imperial, yellow imperial lily)

RIGHT
Fritillaria meleagris (checkered lily, guinea-hen flower)

CLIVIA MINIATA

PRONUNCIATION: KLY-vee-a min-ee-AH-ta
COMMON NAME: Clivia, Lady Clive's lily
HOMELAND: South Africa
HARDINESS: USDA Zones 10–11
SIZE: 2′ tall; 1′–2′ across
INTEREST: Glossy, 1″-wide, strap-shaped, evergreen leaves. Large clusters of dark salmon, funnel-shaped flowers in late winter indoors and spring and early summer outdoors in warm climates.
LIGHT CONDITIONS: Light to dappled shade
SOIL/MOISTURE: Rich, moisture-retentive soil

DESCRIPTION: These showy plants make excellent ground covers for shady places in warm climates. They spread by offsets and require little maintenance, except for slug and snail patrol. Combine with ferns and caladiums. In colder areas, clivias make fine sunroom or greenhouse plants and bloom reliably once they are mature. In fall, after summering outdoors, bring the pot inside to a cool place. Avoid direct sun and keep the soil on the dry side. In mid-winter, buds may begin to show; then move the pot to a sunny, cool window. Cultivars include 'California Sunshine' and 'Dark Red'. Pale yellow-flowered clivias are much sought after, commanding hundreds of dollars.

ERYTHRONIUM TUOLUMNENSE

PRONUNCIATION: e-rith-ROAN-ee-um tu-ol-um-NEN-see
COMMON NAME: Pagoda lily
HOMELAND: Native; California
HARDINESS: USDA Zones 6–8
SIZE: 12″–15″ tall; 15″ across
INTEREST: Shiny, plain, light green leaves. Deep yellow, nodding, lilylike flowers in early to mid-spring, when cherry blossoms bloom.
LIGHT CONDITIONS: Light shade to shade
SOIL/MOISTURE: Well-drained, woodsy soil that does not dry out

DESCRIPTION: Pagoda lily is ideal in spring plantings in woodland areas and mixes well with primroses, lungworts, wood anemones, and trilliums. This species is better known as a parent of the hybrid E. × 'Pagoda', which has wavy-edged leaves, which are sometimes mottled, and several bright yellow flowers per stem.

FRITILLARIA IMPERIALIS 'LUTEA'

PRONUNCIATION: fri-ti-LAH-ree-a im-pe-ree-AH-lis

COMMON NAME: Crown imperial, imperial lily

HOMELAND: Turkey and Iran; cultivar of garden origin

HARDINESS: USDA Zones 5–8

SIZE: 30"–36" tall; 12" across

INTEREST: Dark green, straplike lower foliage, above which rises a stout 2'–3' stem crowned with a tuft of leaves above 3–6 drooping, bell-shaped, yellow flowers. Flowers are brick red in the species.

LIGHT CONDITIONS: Full sun to light shade

SOIL/MOISTURE: Well-drained, fertile soil

DESCRIPTION: Group the bulbs of crown imperial to make an impact; a single bulb, though it seems huge at planting time, usually produces but a single stem. Plant 8–12 together among shrubs or in mixed beds and borders. Since the odor of the leaves reminds many people of cats or skunks, they are seldom used as cut flowers, and perhaps should be sited away from paths and sitting areas. Free from pests, including deer. Planting the bulbs on their side is recommended. Other cultivars in shades of orange and red are available of this species, whose genus also offers many ornamental bulbs. Grown since the 1600s and valuable in period restoration gardens.

FRITILLARIA MELEAGRIS

PRONUNCIATION: fri-ti-LAH-ree-a mel-ee-AH-gris

COMMON NAME: Checkered lily, guinea-hen flower

HOMELAND: Western Europe and British Isles

HARDINESS: USDA Zones 3–8

SIZE: 12"–15" tall; 3" across

INTEREST: Nodding, broadly bell-shaped flowers rise on slender stems in spring, with 1–2 narrow grassy leaves. The unusual flowers are white, heavily veined with reddish purple in a checkerboard pattern.

LIGHT CONDITIONS: Full sun or light to medium shade

SOIL/MOISTURE: Moisture-retentive, organic soil

DESCRIPTION: Checkered lilies are one of the lesser-grown bulbs in American gardens, although they are inexpensive and easy to grow. Select bulbs that are plump and not dried out and shriveled. Naturalize them in damp meadows, or group under low shrubs, where their subtle charm can be appreciated close up. Also suitable for moist rock gardens. The white form 'Alba' is slightly taller and bears pure white flowers.

Narcissus species, hybrids and cultivars (daffodils, jonquils)

Tulipa 'Apricot Beauty' (tulip)

Zantedeschia aethiopica (white calla lily)

LEFT
Lilium 'Stargazer' (lily)

LILIUM 'STARGAZER'

PRONUNCIATION: LIL-ee-um
COMMON NAME: Lily
HOMELAND: Of garden origin
HARDINESS: USDA Zones 4–9
SIZE: 30"–36" tall; 8"–12" across
INTEREST: Fragrant, trumpet-shaped flowers of bold crimson, edged with white, in late summer

LIGHT CONDITIONS: Full sun to light shade
SOIL/MOISTURE: Deep, fertile soil, enriched with leaf mold or compost

DESCRIPTION: Lilies are best grouped between shrubs or perennials in the natural garden. 'Stargazer' combines well with the white flowers of *Echinacea purpurea* 'White Swan', *Salvia farinacea* 'White Porcelain', and *Kalimeris mongolica* [*Asteromoa mongolica*]. Admittedly, 'Stargazer', one of the Oriental hybrid lilies, is bright, but there are numerous other cultivars and species that are more subtle. Look for *L. martagon*, for instance. Plant 6"–8" deep in fall for bloom the following year. They perennialize well and will increase annually. Protect from deer and slugs.

NARCISSUS SPECIES, HYBRIDS AND CULTIVARS

PRONUNCIATION: nar-SISS-us
COMMON NAME: Daffodils, jonquils
HOMELAND: Southwestern Europe, Britain, and North Africa
HARDINESS: USDA Zones 4–8
SIZE: 3"–24" tall in bloom; 2"–6" across
INTEREST: Late-winter- and spring-blooming flowers mostly in yellows, white, and sometimes pink. The flowers have a "cup" or "trumpet," the perianth, which may be a different color from the "petals," or corolla.

LIGHT CONDITIONS: Full sun to light deciduous shade
SOIL/MOISTURE: Evenly moist, fertile soil that drains well

DESCRIPTION: With careful selection, there are daffodils appropriate for every garden setting from the smallest species, such as *N. asturiensis* or 'Midget' for the rock garden, and the bold, white-flowered 'Mt. Hood' or golden 'Carlton' for formal bedding areas. Daffodils are superb as an underplanting for shrubs and deciduous trees in light woodland areas, and are especially good combined with daylilies and other later-blooming perennials that can hide the fading daffodil foliage. Plant the bulbs (which are not attacked by deer or rodents) in fall to flower the following spring.

TULIPA 'APRICOT BEAUTY'

PRONUNCIATION: **TEW-li-pa**
COMMON NAME: **Tulip**
HOMELAND: **Of garden origin**
HARDINESS: **USDA Zones 2–8**
SIZE: **15"–18" tall; 6" across**
INTEREST: **Bright, deep apricot flowers in** **mid- to late spring**
LIGHT CONDITIONS: **Full sun to very light shade**
SOIL/MOISTURE: **Rich, moisture-retentive soil, amended with very well rotted manure, compost, or leaf mold**

DESCRIPTION: 'Apricot Beauty' is one of the best-known tulips in American gardens. It is listed in catalogs under the Triumph tulips, which are derived from the Early Single types crossed with the Darwins. They force well indoors and are spectacular massed in formal gardens, but they are equally at home planted in drifts in light deciduous woodland or open areas in a natural garden setting. (In light shade, their color is paler, perhaps more pleasing.) In cold zones, plant deeply to encourage perennializing; in the South, expect to replace them every 2–3 years, even in natural areas.

ZANTEDESCHIA AETHIOPICA

PRONUNCIATION: **zan-te-DESH-ee-a aye-thee-OH-pi-ka**
COMMON NAME: **White calla lily**
HOMELAND: **South Africa**
HARDINESS: **USDA Zones 8–10**
SIZE: **To 3' tall; 12"–24" across**
INTEREST: **Showy flowers, composed of a pure** **white spathe surrounding an erect creamy spadix. Long-stemmed dark green foliage, arrow- or lance-shaped.**
LIGHT CONDITIONS: **Partial shade**
SOIL/MOISTURE: **Moist, rich to average soil, or in muck in water**

DESCRIPTION: Widely grown in mild regions, calla lilies are magnificent when allowed to naturalize at the water's edge. Combine them with yellow circle flower (*Lysimachia punctata*) for a cool yellow-and-white medley. The smaller cultivar 'Childsiana' blooms more freely, and it makes a good container plant in greenhouses and sunrooms. Yellow-blooming *Z. elliotiana* and pink-flowered *Z. rehmannii* are suitable for small garden pools and ponds. Several hybrid cultivars are available in shades of lavender, yellow, and red as well as white. Grown commercially as a cut flower.

Grasses and Grasslike Plants

Grasses and Grasslike Plants

Most of the plants we know and love are technically dicotyledons. That is, when they first sprout from seeds, two seed leaves emerge from the ground. Some other plants, however, are monocotyledons: only one leaf comes up, which looks like a blade of grass (and often is). These grasses—and look-alikes such as sedges or rushes—add a powerful, impressive, and unmistakable architectural accent to plantings, from the tallest revenna, at 12 feet, to the tiny ophiopogons, some of which are a few inches tall—and may be black! Grasses and grasslike plants are currently hot in horticulture, perhaps because these "new" ornamentals make this unparalleled statement in the garden.

When you need a botanical exclamation point, grasses and grasslike plants can do it—by the swimming pool (or in the garden pool); sparking the billowy masses of flowering perennials; reiterating the permanent landscape elements such as a house, paved space, or sculpture. The grasses are living sculptures, seeming very natural—nearly wild—and yet with an almost unreal presence and symmetry.

Look down and you'll see ground covers besides grass lawn. There's *Liriope*, or lily turf, a wonderful and nearly indestructable grass imitator that blooms not with dry flowers and seeds on plumes, but with grape hyacinthlike blue or white flowers followed by black berries. This is a useful plant for edging a planting bed or lining a path—especially in shade.

You might think that grasses and their allies are perfect plants, but many self-sow and others can get out of hand. Grasses in nature colonize great swaths of open land and that's what they would like to do in your backyard. Most *Miscanthus*, or maiden grass, self-sow in zone 7 and southward, but *M. sinensis* 'Purpurascens' does not.

I am always looking for native grasses, since, if they self-sow, at least it may be into a community to which they already belong. They probably have a symbiotic relationship with some animal who eats them, or another natural balance to prevent their taking over the universe. Native *Panicum virgatum*, panic or switch grass, has lovely arching habit with silvery-blue blades tinged with red and airy purple flowers held above the foliage.

Chasmanthium latifolium (northern sea oats, spangle grass)

Liriope muscari 'Variegata' (variegated blue lilyturf)

Miscanthus sinensis 'Zebrinus' (zebra grass, banded miscanthus)

LEFT
Miscanthus sinensis 'Gracillimus' (maiden grass)

CHASMANTHIUM LATIFOLIUM

PRONUNCIATION: kas-MAN-thee-um lat-ih-FOL-ee-um

COMMON NAME: Northern sea oats, spangle grass

HOMELAND: South, central, and eastern North America

HARDINESS: USDA Zones 5–9

SIZE: 2'–3' tall; 1' across

INTEREST: Light green, grassy leaves that turn copper in fall and brown in winter. Flat flower spikes that brown and persist well into winter.

LIGHT CONDITIONS: Partial shade

SOIL/MOISTURE: Moisture-retentive, rich to average soil

DESCRIPTION: Clump-forming northern sea oats is a beautiful grass over a very long season. Upright in the spring, the foliage mixes well with early perennials; later on, its habit relaxes when it comes into flower, and it takes a more prominent position in the border. A good container plant, and also sought after in the cutting garden. Its tolerance of salty conditions makes it an ideal choice for seaside gardens. Interplant clumps of it among bright impatiens and other annuals. Cut down in late winter or early spring; a stand of it is a beautiful sight dusted with winter snow.

LIRIOPE MUSCARI 'VARIEGATA'

PRONUNCIATION: le-RYE-o-pee (le-REE-o-pee) mus-KAH-ree

COMMON NAME: Variegated blue lilyturf

HOMELAND: China and Japan; cultivar of garden origin

HARDINESS: USDA Zones 5–9

SIZE: 15"–24" tall; 12"–18" across

INTEREST: Evergreen straplike leaves, variegated with white with green stripes; the species has dark green foliage. Spikes of small purple hyacinth-like flowers in late summer followed by black berries.

LIGHT CONDITIONS: Sun to shade

SOIL/MOISTURE: Well-drained, average soil

DESCRIPTION: Lilyturf is one of the most widely used plants for ground cover, especially in warm climates. The variegated sorts do not tolerate intense sun well and prefer some shade, but variegated 'Silvery Sunproof', 12"–15" tall, is reputedly a sun-tolerant cultivar. Excellent massed with hostas, astilbes, epimediums, and ferns in low-maintenance, shaded areas. The variegated sorts are especially valuable in winter gardens, where their white-and-green leaves enliven the dark days. 'Munroe's White', 12"–15" tall, has white flowers and solid green leaves; 'Big Blue', 8"–12" tall, bears violet flowers. Mow to the ground in early spring to allow new growth to develop. Beware of slugs and snails.

MISCANTHUS SINENSIS 'GRACILLIMUS'

PRONUNCIATION: mis-KAN-thus si-NEN-sis
COMMON NAME: Maiden grass
HOMELAND: Eastern Asia; cultivar of garden origin
HARDINESS: USDA Zones 5–9
SIZE: 5'–6' tall; 3'–4' across

INTEREST: Thick clumps of slender light green leaves highlighted by a white midrib. Airy 7' spikes of coppery or pinkish white flowers in early fall, followed by winter color.
LIGHT CONDITIONS: Full sun to light shade
SOIL/MOISTURE: Well-drained, average soil

DESCRIPTION: One of the first cultivars to gain popularity as Americans rediscover ornamental grasses, maiden grass is now widely grown. Its fall color varies according to climate, but it is always attractive, even in winter. In flower beds and borders, maiden grass is not too large to combine well with late-summer asters, boltonias, and Japanese anemones. It also softens and highlights somber evergreens to good effect. Do not plant adjacent to meadow areas in warm climates, as this plant self-sows.

MISCANTHUS SINENSIS 'ZEBRINUS'

PRONUNCIATION: mis-KAN-thus si-NEN-sis
COMMON NAME: Zebra grass, banded miscanthus
HOMELAND: Eastern Asia; cultivar of garden origin
HARDINESS: USDA Zones 6–9
SIZE: 6'–8' tall; 3'–4' across

INTEREST: Clumps of arching leaves, banded horizontally with yellow by summer. In fall, coppery spikes of flowers rise 1'–2' above the mass of foliage.
LIGHT CONDITIONS: Full sun to light shade
SOIL/MOISTURE: Well-drained, average soil

DESCRIPTION: Zebra grass makes an impressive accent plant in a container, beside a rock outcropping, among foundation plantings, or to punctuate a mixed flower bed or border. Combine it with colorful perennials all summer long, and allow it to remain standing until crushed by snow or rain in winter. Mass beside water so that the reflection is visible. If not in full sun, the plant will flop.

Panicum virgatum
(switch grass)

Pennisetum setaceum
'Rubrum' (purple
fountain grass)

Typha angustifolia (narrow-
leaf cattail, soft flag)

RIGHT
Pennisetum alopecuroides
(fountain grass)

PANICUM VIRGATUM

PRONUNCIATION: PAN-ik-um veer-GAH-tum

COMMON NAME: Switch grass

HOMELAND: Canada to Florida, eastern seaboard west to the Rockies

HARDINESS: USDA Zones 5–9

SIZE: 4'–7' tall; 18"–24" across

INTEREST: Clumps of sturdy stems, clothed in deep green or grayish foliage. Airy sprays with a profusion of minute flowers in midsummer. Good fall color.

LIGHT CONDITIONS: Full sun to very light shade

SOIL/MOISTURE: Moist, rich soil, but tolerant of most

DESCRIPTION: Excellent massed beside streams or ponds and for controlling erosion. In the garden it is ideal in transition areas, where it provides food for wildlife. A good dried cut flower for winter arrangements. Plant it among shrubs and foundation plantings; especially attractive in front of variegated-leaved red-stem dogwood or weigela. Reddish 'Haense Herms' and stiff blue-green 'Heavy Metal' are popular compact cultivars. Exceptional native grass.

PENNISETUM ALOPECUROIDES

PRONUNCIATION: pen-ih-SEE-tum al-oh-pek-yur-OY-deez

COMMON NAME: Fountain grass

HOMELAND: Eastern Asia, Australia

HARDINESS: USDA Zones 6–9

SIZE: Mound of foliage 2'–3' tall and as wide

INTEREST: Handsome narrow foliage makes a dense clump, bright green during the growing season and turning tan and buff in late fall. Foxtaillike flower spikes are carried on arching 3'–4' stems in late summer and persist well into winter.

LIGHT CONDITIONS: Full sun

SOIL/MOISTURE: Moist, fertile soil that drains well

DESCRIPTION: Fountain grass makes a splendid foil for brightly colored annuals and perennials in mixed plantings, but is also attractive massed in open spaces. Excellent in containers and mixed with shrubs in foundation plantings, where its winter interest is valuable. Good for cutting both fresh and dried. The finer-textured cultivar 'Hameln' grows under 20" tall and prefers northern conditions. 'Moudry' has coarser, less arching foliage than the species, with startling black flower spikes. Suitable for the rock garden, dwarf 'Little Bunny' grows only 10"–12" tall.

PENNISETUM SETACEUM 'RUBRUM' ['Cupreum']

PRONUNCIATION: pen-ih-SEE-tum seh-TAY-see-um

COMMON NAME: Purple fountain grass

HOMELAND: Of garden origin

HARDINESS: USDA Zones 9–10

SIZE: 3'–4' tall and as wide

INTEREST: Arching clumps of reddish bur-gundy leaves, topped with persistent buff- and wine-colored flower plumes from midsummer to frost

LIGHT CONDITIONS: Full sun

SOIL/MOISTURE: Well-drained but moisture-retentive, fertile soil

DESCRIPTION: This popular grass is treated as an annual north of Zone 9. It is elegant as a container plant, perhaps combined with trailing pink petunias or verbenas. Attractive contrasted with silver artemisias, dusty miller, or lamb's ears, but also stunning against red-leaved cannas, purple-leaved 'Crimson Pygmy' barberry, or 'Velvet Cloak' smokebush; even purple-leaved basil or perilla makes a good textural, monochromatic companion. Good in coastal gardens and as a dried flower. There is a compact dwarf form.

TYPHA ANGUSTIFOLIA

PRONUNCIATION: TY-fah an-gus-ti-FOL-ee-a

COMMON NAME: Narrow-leaf cattail, soft flag

HOMELAND: Worldwide

HARDINESS: USDA Zones 5–9

SIZE: 3'–5' tall and as wide or wider

INTEREST: Dense clumps of erect, $1/2''$–$3/4''$ sword-shaped leaves. Chocolate cigar-shaped flower spikes from midsummer persist.

LIGHT CONDITIONS: Full sun to light shade

SOIL/MOISTURE: Deep, fertile soil beneath 6''–12'' of standing water

DESCRIPTION: Narrow-leaf cattail is excellent planted along the edges of earth-bottom ponds to prevent bank erosion. The soft blades arch and sway in the breeze, but the plants spread to create large stands, which must be controlled with a root barrier. However, this species is small enough to plant in small tubs and water gardens and is often combined with water lilies and water irises. A good plant to provide cover for wildlife, and also a source of food for muskrats and other water animals. Striking as a cut flower, fresh or dried.

Appendix

Mail-Order
Nurseries

Ambergate Gardens
8015 Krey Avenue
Waconia, MN 55387
(612) 443-2248
*Hostas, unusual perennials, Martagon
lilies. Catalog: $2*

Anderson Iris Gardens
22179 Keather Avenue North
Forest Lake, MN 55025
(612) 433-5268
Bearded iris, peonies. Catalog: $1

Andre Viette Farm & Nursery
Route 1, Box 16
State Route 608
Fishersville, VA 22939
(703) 943-2315
*Huge list including many
   perennials classified for shade.
   Catalog: $2*

Antique Rose Emporium
Route 5, Box 143
Brenham, TX 77833
(409) 836-9051
Old garden roses. Catalog: $5

Appalachian Gardens
P.O. Box 82
Waynesboro, PA 17268
(717) 762-4312
*Conifers, flowering shrubs, trees.
   Catalog: $2*

Arborvillage Farm Nursery
P.O. Box 227
Holt, MO 64048
(816) 264-3911
*Flowering shrubs, trees.
   Catalog: $1*

Arrowhead Alpines
P.O. Box 857
Flowerville, MI 48836
(517) 223-3581
*Several plant and seed lists for conifers,
wildflowers, ferns, alpines.
Catalog: $2*

Arthur H. Steffen, Inc.
P.O. Box 184
1259 Fairport Road
Fairport, NY 14450
Vines, especially clematis. Catalog: $2

Bluestone Perennials
7211 Middle Ridge Road
Madison, OH 44057
(800) 952-5243
*Inexpensive seedlings in flats
(3, 6, 12, etc.), 400 varieties.
Catalog: free*

Brand Peony Farm
P.O. Box 842
Saint Cloud, MN 56302
*Peonis, especially heirloom varieties.
Catalog: $1*

Bundles of Bulbs
112 Green Springs Valley Road
Owings Mills, MD 21117
(301) 363-1371
Spring-flowering bulbs. Catalog: $2

Busse Gardens
Route 2, Box 238
Cokato, MN 55321
(612) 286-2654
Hard-to-find perennials. Catalog: $2

California Carnivores
7020 Trenton-Healdsburg
Road
Forestville, CA 95436
(707) 838-1630

Canyon Creek Nursery
3527 Dry Creek Road
Oroville, CA 95965
(919) 533-2166
*Herbaceous perennials, salvias, and
geraniums. Catalog: $2*

Caprice Nursery
15425 Southwest Pleasant Hill
Road
Sherwood, OR 97140
(503) 625-7241
*Peonies, Japanese and Siberian irises,
Hemerocallis, hostas. Catalog: $2*

Carroll Gardens
P.O. Box 310
444 East main Street
Westminster, MD 21157
(800) 638-6334
*Extensive, well-written catalog.
Catalog: $2*

Christa's Cactus
529 West Pima
Coolidge, AZ 85228
(602) 723-4185
*Desert trees, shrubs, succulents, cacti.
Catalog: $1*

Collector's Nursery
16408 Northeast 102d Avenue
Battle Ground, WA 98684
(206) 574-3832
*Unusual conifers, flowering shrubs,
trees, herbaceous perennials, vines,
alpines, dwarf conifers, Gentiana,
Tricyrtis, species Iris. Catalog: $2*

Colorado Alpines
P.O. Box 2708
Avon, CO 81620
(303) 949-6464
*Dwarf conifers, alpines, native shrubs,
trees, plants of the West. Catalog: $2*

Country Wetlands Nursery
P.O. Box 337
Muskego, WI 53150
(414) 679-1268
*Native aquatic, wetland, and bog
plants, sedges. Catalog: $1*

Crownsville Nursery
P.O. Box 797
Crownsville, MD 21032
(301) 923-2212
*Outstanding list with good descrip-
tions; hosta and familiar and
unusual perennials. Catalog: $2*

Daffodil Mart
Route 3, Box 794
Glouster, VA 23061
(804) 693-6339
*Vast list of narcissus varieties; also
tulips, crocuses, alliums, and other
bulbs. Catalog: $1*

Desert Nursery
1301 South Copper Street
Deming, NM 88030
(505) 546-6264
*Succulents and hardy cacti. List:
long SASE*

Eastern Plant Specialties
P.O. Box 226
Georgetown, ME 04548
(207) 371-2888
*Dwarf conifers, flowering shrubs,
trees, rhododendrons, kalmia, azalea. Catalog: $2*

Eco-Gardens
P.O. Box 1227
Decatur, GA 30031
(404) 294-6468
*Native eastern wildflowers, trees,
shrubs, ferns, and exotics.
Catalog: $2*

Forestfarm
990 Tetherow Road
Williams, OR 97544
(503) 846-6963
*Excellent source of woody natives and
unusual plants. Informative catalog is
one of the best sources. Catalog: $3*

The Fragrant Path
P.O. Box 328
Fort Calhoun, NE 68023
*Fragrant perennials, annuals, herbs,
vines (rare and heirloom).
Catalog: $2*

Garden Place
P.O. Box 388
Mentor, OH 44061-0388
(216) 255-3705
Ground covers, perennials, grasses.
   Catalog: $1

Gossler Farms Nursery
1200 Weaver Road
Springfield, OR 97478-9663
(503) 746-3922 or 747-0749
Magnolias and stewartia; 200–300
   varieties of plants. Catalog: $1

Greer Gardens
1280 Goodpasture Island Road
Eugene, OR 97401-1794
(503) 686-8266
Excellent source of rhododendrons;
   extensive list of Japanese maples
   and rare shrubs. Catalog: $3

Heard Gardens, Ltd.
5355 Merle Hay Road
Johnston, IA 50131
(515) 276-4533
Lilacs. Catalog: $2

Heaths and Heathers
P.O. Box 850
1199 Monte-Elma Road
Elma, WA 98541
(206) 482-3258
Heaths and heathers. List:
   long SASE

Heronswood Nursery, Ltd.
7530 288th Street NE
Kingston, WA 98346
(206) 297-4172
Conifers, flowering shrubs, trees,
   herbaceous plants. Catalog: $3

Joy Creek Nursery
20300 Northwest Watson
   Road
Scappoose, OR 97056
(503) 543-7474
Shrubs, herbaceous perennials, alpines,
   grasses. Catalog: $2

Klehm Nursery
4210 North Duncan Road
Champagne, IL 61821
(800) 553-3715
Herbaceous perennials, ferns, Siberian
   iris, Hemerocallis, hostas, peonies.
   Catalog: $4

Lamb Nurseries
East 101 Sharp Avenue
Spokane, WA 99202
(509) 328-7956
Perennials for shade. Catalog: free

Lamtree Farm
2323 Copeland Road
Warrensville, NC 28693
(910) 385-6144
Native propagated trees and shrubs:
   Franklinia, Stewartia, Styrax,
   Halesia, Rhododendron,
   Azalea, Kalmia. *Catalog: $2*

Louisiana Nursery
Route 7, Box 43
Opelousas, LA 70570
(318) 948-3696
Catalogs: $6 magnolias, perennials,
  and woody plants; $4 iris and
  Hemerocallis; *$3.50 fruiting*
  trees, shrubs, and vines; $3
  hydrangea; $3 bamboos and orna-
  mental grasses; $2 Clivia list;
  $25 for all

Maple Tree Gardens
P.O. Box 547
Ponca, NE 68770-0547
(402) 755-2615
Maple trees, bearded iris,
  Hemerocallis, *hosta.*
  Catalog: $1

Maryland Aquatic Nurseries
3427 North Furnace Road
Jarrettsville, MD 21084
Native bog and water plants and oth-
  ers. Catalog: free

Mary's Plant Farm
2410 Lanes Mill Road
Hamilton, OH 45013
(513) 892-2055
Flowering shrubs, perennials, ferns,
  iris, grasses, native plants.
  Catalog: $1

McClure & Zimmerman
P.O. Box 368
108 West Winnebago
Friesland, WI 53935
(414) 326-4220
Netherlands importers; good quality
  bulbs. Catalog: free

Moon Mountain Wildflowers
P.O. Box 34
864 Napa Avenue
Morro Bay, CA 93442-0032
(805) 772-2473
Seeds, supplies, and books on wild-
  flowers. Catalog: $1

Oak Hill Farm
204 Pressly Street
Clover, SC 29710
(803) 222-4245
Hardy evergreens, species
  rhododendrons. Catalog: free

Old House Garden
526 Third Street
Ann Arbor, MI 48103-4957
(313) 995-1486
Heirloom bulbs. Catalog: $1

Owens Farms
Route 3, Box 158-A
Curve-Nankipoo Road
Ripley, TN 38063
(901) 635-1588
Native deciduous hollies.
  Catalog: $2

Prairie Nursery
Route I, Box 365
Westfield, WI 53964
(608) 296-3679
Meadow and waterside plants.
Catalog: $2

Paradise Water Gardens
62 May Street
Whitman, MA 02382
(617) 447-4711
General water-garden supplier.
Catalog: $3

Roslyn Nursery
211 Burrs Lane
Dix Hills, NY 11746
(516) 643-9347
Extensive catalog of rare and familiar
woody plants, rhododendrons,
pieris, kalmias, azaleas.
Catalog: $2

Russell Graham
4030 Eagle Crest Road NW
Salem, OR 97304
(503) 362-1135
Wonderful collection of ferns, shade
plants, and bulbs. Catalog: $2

S. Sherer & Sons
104 Waterside Road
Northport, NY 11768
(516) 261-7432
Complete supplies, colocasias and giant
taros, third generation. Catalog: free

Siskiyou Rare Plant Nursery
2825 Cummings Road
Medford, OR 97501
(503) 772-6846
Dwarf conifers; dwarf shrubs and
trees; alpine, rock, woodland
plants; hardy ferns. Catalog: $2

Sunlight Gardens
Route I, Box 600-A
Andersonville, TN 37705
(615) 494-8237
Shade perennials, too. Catalog: $2

Tranquil Lake Nursery
45 River Street
Rehobeth, MA 02769-1359
Hemerocallis, *Japanese and*
Siberian iris. Catalog: $1

Waterford Gardens
74 East Allendale Road
Saddle River, NJ 07458
(201) 327-0721
Aquatic plants, water lilies, lotuses.
Catalog: $5

Wedge Nursery
Route 2, Box 114
Albert Lea, MN 56007
(507) 373-5225
Lilacs. Catalog: free

White Flower Farm
Route 63
Litchfield, CT 06759
(203) 567-0801
Wonderful catalog, great information.
Catalog: $5

Wicklein's Water Gardens
P.O. Box 9780
Baldwin, MD 21013
(410) 823-1335
Aquatic and bog plants.
Catalog: $2

Gilbert H. Wild & Son, Inc.
P.O. Box 338
1112 Joplin Street
Sarcoxie, MO 64862-0338
(417) 548-3514
Hemerocallis, *iris, peonies.*
Catalog: $3

Woodlanders, Inc.
1128 Colleton Avenue
Aiken, SC 29801
(803) 648-7522
Native trees and shrubs and some
herbaceous perennials. Catalog: free

Yucca Do Nursery
P.O. Box 655
Waller, TX 77484-0655
(409) 826-6363
Texas and southwestern natives and
conifers, flowering shrubs.
Catalog: $4

Front cover: *Oenothera fruticosa*. **Title** page: rock garden perennials. Contents page (clockwise from top left): *Centaurea cyanus* and *Coreopsis tinctoria*; hybrid rhododendrons; *Pennisetum alopercuroides*; *Achillea filipendulina*; *Wisteria*. p. 10: *Papaver rhoeas* with *Centaurea cyanus*. p.11: *Nymphaea*. **Annuals** chapter opener (clockwise from top left): *Lychnis coronaria*; *Cosmos bipinnatus*; *Catharanus roseus*; *Tropaeolum nanum*; *Digitalis purpurea*; *Centaurea cyanus*, *Coreopsis tinctoria*, and *Chrysanthemum leucanthemum*; center photo: *Daucus carota* var. *carota*. **Perennials** chapter opener (clockwise from top left): *Dicentra spectabilis* and *Senecio cineraria* 'Siver Dust'; *Mertensia virginica*; *Nelumbo nucifera* 'Alba Grandiflora'; *Rudbeckia hirta*; *Paeonia lactiflora* 'Santa Fe'; *Lysichiton americanum*; center photo:*Papaver orientale* 'Helen Elizabeth'. **Shrubs** chapter opener (clockwise from top left): *Syringa vulgaris*; *Euonymus alatus*; *Pittosporum tobira* 'Variegatum'; hydrangea; *Lavandula angustifolia*; an evergreen planting. **Vines** chapter opener (clockwise from top left): *Hedera helix* and *Parthenocissus tricupidata*; *Passiflora incense*; *Clematis paniculata*; *Polygonum aubertii*; landscape rose 'The Fairy'; *Ipomoea alba*; *Hedera colchina* 'Dentata Variegata'; center photo: *Wisteria*. Bulbs chapter opener (clockwise from top left): *Narcissus* spp.; *Lilium tigrinum*; *Sparaxix tricolor*; azalea shrubs and *Narcissus* spp.; tulips; center photo: *Zantedeschia aethiopica*. **Grasses and Grass-like Plants** chapter opener (clockwise from top left): *Pennisetum alopecuroides*; a prairie; sedum 'Autumn Joy' and *Pennisetum alopecuroides*; *Panicum virgatum*; *Miscanthus saccariflorus*, *Pennisetum alopecuoides*, *Calamagrostis acutiflora stricta*, and *Rudbeckia hirta*; *Calamagrostis* spp. and miscanthus; *Miscanthus sinensis* 'Variegata'; *agrostis nebulosa*; center photo: *Miscanthus saccariflorus*. **Appendix** opener: *Aconitum carmichaelii*; *Aquilegia* hybrid, *Phlox divaricata*, and *Myosotis alpestris*; *Nymphaea* x *marliacea*; *Rosa rugosa*; *Thermopsis caroliniana*; center photo: *Nymphaea* 'Wood's White Knight'. p. 122: *Aquilegia* hybrid. p. 127: *Euphorbia characias.*

U.S. Plant Hardiness Zones: Approximate range of average annual minimum temperatures (F°): zone 1: below -50°; zone 2: -50° to -40°; zone 3: -40° to -30°; zone 4: -30° to -20°; zone 5: -20° to -10°; zone 6: -10° to 0°; zone 7: 0° to 10°; zone 8: 10° to 20°; zone 9: 20° to 30°; zone 10: 30° to 40°